August 2020

D0834259

THE
JOURNEY
OF A SMALL
TOWN GIRL

EMILY SZAJDA

With joy & blessings—
All the best always!

Black Rose Writing | Texas

©2020 by Emily Szajda

All rights reserved. No part of this book may be reproduced, stored in a retrieval system or transmitted in any form or by any means without the prior written permission of the publishers, except by a reviewer who may quote brief passages in a review to be printed in a newspaper, magazine or journal.

The author grants the final approval for this literary material.

First printing

Some names and identifying details may have been changed to protect the privacy of individuals.

ISBN: 978-1-68433-411-7
PUBLISHED BY BLACK ROSE WRITING
www.blackrosewriting.com

Printed in the United States of America
Suggested Retail Price (SRP) $19.95

Big Time Journey of a Small Town Girl is printed in Sabon

*As a planet-friendly publisher, Black Rose Writing does its best to eliminate unnecessary waste to reduce paper usage and energy costs, while never compromising the reading experience. As a result, the final word count vs. page count may not meet common expectations.

Photography by Anna Paprocka
Editing by Gay Walley

BIG
TIME
JOURNEY
OF A SMALL
TOWN GIRL

PREFACE

WISDOM IS BEST SHARED

I am a firm believer in the idea that the power of wisdom derives from our ability to share it.

While wisdom may have nothing to do with intellectual capacity, it does have a lot to do with how we navigate our lives. It is the knowledge we gain by simply living and experiencing life, which no academic institution can adequately do justice to.

While traditional knowledge is thought to come from those who came before us, everyone that you come in contact with, young and old, has their own story to tell. Through the sharing of our knowledge and our experiences, we feel more empathy for those around us, and we gain insight into how to circumvent some of life's most significant challenges.

Wisdom is not achieved by following a road map, but rather through our own agency. Think about mentors in your life, past and present, that have shaped your perception of reality. Without their influence, our view of the world around us would be limited.

There is no doubt that we have all had our share of ups and downs. Yet, without reaching out to family and, a community of like-minded individuals, we would feel alone. Our feelings and experiences would get buried and lost, and we would feel disconnected from all that surrounds us. By sharing our wisdom, we are able to build richer relationships based on acceptance and compassion. As humans, we are not so different from one another. It is only when we acknowledge this fact that we can actually show up and support one another in ways that have consequence.

I have had many mentors in my life and mention a few by name in this book. Without these individuals, and the ones not mentioned, that shared intimate experiences with me, would I be able to tell my story. I hope that by sharing my wisdom, you can find resonance.

HOW THIS BOOK WORKS

Every chapter in this book is a story, periods of my life that induced growth. It wasn't until I learned everything I needed to was I actually able to sit and write in length about my experiences.

Coming from Victor, Iowa, somewhere along the way I knew I wanted to venture away from the small farming community that had shaped me. I wanted to see the world and grow in a way that I couldn't if I stayed. While residing close to family and living not far from where we grew up, my old friend from high school, Ellie Hawkins, encouraged me on my quest to cultivate a new understanding of the world and an appreciation of my place in it. After an extended period of traveling abroad, having backpacked all over Europe, Ellie sent me a message. Having lived vicariously through my photographs on social media, she said to me, I can imagine you writing a book called Big Time Journey of a Small Town Girl, hence the title.

Through introspection and the incorporation of mindfulness I have developed over time, I share key take-aways from my life's journey. These capstone pieces are meant to be that nugget of wisdom at the end of each chapter you can reflect on and employ in your own life.

PROLOGUE

"Every dreamer knows it is entirely possible to be homesick for a place you've never been to, perhaps more homesick than for familiar ground."
-Judith Thurman

"I have no idea where we are," was all that I could think as I turned down yet another passageway leading in a direction that I knew didn't seem quite right. Through a series of twists and turns down ancient streets and tiny back alleys, I reluctantly donned the white flag. I was lost. Trying to retrace my footsteps along cobblestone streets, I realized I may have let my guard down, not paying adequate attention to the landmarks that, like bread-crumbs, could lead us back to our tour group's meeting point. Who knew that Sienna's historical city center was a labyrinth of secret passages and remote corners, red brick buildings offering little way of distinguishing one from another? Each building embodied centuries of history within its walls. Breathtaking of course, but timeless beauty and eternal charm didn't offer any aid when what we really needed was a map.

I didn't know why I kept trying to decipher Italian, as I stared up at the street names etched into white stone tiles. The street of the merchants, the street for the tailors, they all made little sense to me as we strayed deeper into the heart of the old city center, a maze of picturesque Roman ways, which only the locals could navigate without wandering off course. We had drifted away from the rest of our large tour group in hopes of finding fresh fruit from a small local stall nestled down some cozy corridor leading to yet another primitive artifact or ornate façade.

Laura and I had sought a light lunch. Sweltering temperatures caused beads of sweat to drip from my brow. In this heat, it was hard to imagine joining the others for the pre-ordered three-course meal that would, of course, include a plate of delectable handmade pasta with a mouthwatering sauce of tomatoes so fresh that you could taste the warmth of the Tuscan sun nurturing the vine. The Italian kitchen has no rival. Yes, the French could contend that their cuisine is more sophisticated with the likes of Escoffier and Paul Bocuse, but for me, if I were tempted to indulge in fresh pasta every day, I would never tire. Not to mention I haven't the slightest will to pass up Italian desserts, homemade tiramisu, panna cotta and gelato made of toasted pistachios, all so satisfying it's difficult to show any self-restraint. But we didn't indulge in sweets. With an hour set aside for lunch, our agenda was on schedule, leaving us no time for the wise and much admired afternoon siesta required after such a feast. We were on a guided wine tour through the sumptuous Tuscan countryside, for goodness sake. Why fill up on carbs when there were more tantalizing elixirs to indulge in?

Back to our conquest to find a bundle of succulent grapes, the fruit of the gods, as though Tellus, the Roman god of the earth, would miraculously emerge and satisfy our meager request. A relatively easy task considering we were in Italy. You would think there were open-air markets on every street corner, but this romanticized image was not reality. We searched high and low, asking merchants and locals only to be pointed in some far off direction away from the bustling crowds of tourists. Finally, we arrived at the prize, a local shop stocked full of regional produce. The old man behind the counter shuffled his feet, taking his time as we patiently waited. He tied up the bundles of grapes in two brown paper bags, and as we paid, Laura looked at her wristwatch. Such a simple task had taken much longer than anticipated. Slowly we came to realize, looking around at the tenderly kept houses with tiny window boxes full of bright blooms, we hadn't the slightest idea how to get back to the groups' meeting point.

In all my travels, I could proudly say I have never gotten lost, not truly lost at least, up until now.

But as the sun beat down on our naked shoulders, even lost, we took a moment to grab a handful of grapes, so perfect in both shape and color, a vibrant hue of violet so exquisite that when biting into the tender flesh, the grape released a sweetness that can only be likened to the divine. The delicate taste of summer forever lingered on my lips.

It is occasions like these that make life worth living. This was the epiphany that I had reached after the thousands of miles I had traveled and the numerous countries I had visited. It doesn't matter where you are from or where exactly you are going, but the details, the stories in between the lines make the bigger picture more complete. I wasn't ready to head back and face reality. I liked it out here, even if I wasn't quite sure where here was exactly.

I had set out on this grand adventure months ago on a quest for self-discovery, similar to so many others. I wasn't the first, nor would I be the last woman seeking refuge from a devastating heartbreak. I wasn't trying to run into the arms of another man, to be swooped off my feet in yet another relationship. I knew that would only be a Band-

Aid covering up the larger wound, and that it would never properly fix the damage that had been done. I had needed this time out on my own to regain that sense of self that I inherently lost when our relationship came to an abrupt end.

Getting lost in Tuscany was in short, a comedic parody of my life at the moment. For months, I had been carelessly gallivanting around Europe with no compass to guide me. It was a complete change from the life I had once known managing fine dining restaurants and working for a prominent resort back in the United States. From a very young age, I had been taught to be the responsible type, never the vagabond. My father had instilled these ethics in me, having been led by his example. He taught me to work hard and that in doing so, I would be successful. In Phoenix, Arizona, my last residence before taking the time to travel, I was considered the woman in-the-know, educated, successful and driven.

That is until I woke up unexpectedly one day from the daze I was living in to find I was nothing like that girl I used to know. I had been dating a man for nearly five years, and somewhere in the midst of falling head-over-heels in love, I started to lose the drive for greatness that I had once possessed. When I found myself on the losing end of a horrible relationship that was stained with lies and deceit, it was too late. The harm had already been done. I was no longer following the path I had intended to be on. I had realistic dreams. I wanted to earn my postgraduate degree, to live abroad, and to someday own my own business. But somewhere I wandered astray, and every day seemed like the same old routine, an anticlimactic scene from the movie Groundhog Day.

Being lost had a whole new meaning. I had hit a crossroads in my life, and there was no turning back. I had to move on and press forward, start living more fully. What that meant I hadn't the slightest clue. I just knew I had to be selfish for a while. For the greater part of our relationship, I had given of myself for the betterment of the relationship without asking anything in return. I was tired and felt I had been mistreated. The time had come that I needed to reinvest in myself, to put myself first.

Instead of losing myself figuratively in a relationship, I needed to lose myself in the world. I needed to remove myself from the comforts of home, of security and complacency in order to discover what made me tick, what motivated me.

When Laura and I found ourselves in this silly quandary that day in Sienna, I found myself laughing. A quest for fruit, go figure. I asked to roam free, to get lost in the world and sure enough, the universe handed it to me on a silver Etruscan platter. Don't go throwing wishes around, choose wisely, and be more objective, the universe was saying.

We were short on time and far from finding our way, but hey, there were alternatives. Catching the tour would be the easiest and most productive. All I knew was that I didn't want to miss out on an indulgent afternoon of sipping wine in one of the most renowned regions of the world. A girl has to have priorities, right?! Taking the train wasn't for me. I was on a mission; the wine enthusiast inside me would not miss out on her share of the lot. Laura was on the same page, fairly cool-headed, so we started to make progress. Reaching for the red headsets, we had stashed away in our purses, it was clear that we still might make the tour. Sporting the not-so-fashionable headset in Italy was the least of our concerns. What mattered most was that we were starting to think more strategically about how to overcome the misadventure we found ourselves in.

The signal was faint; we looked like that guy on the television commercial advertising cell phones, "Can you hear me now?" but there wasn't anyone on the other end of the line. Maybe, just maybe the guided tour had already started, and we would soon be in broadcast range. This would be the much-needed clue to complete the puzzle. The whole afternoon felt like this staged performance that was meant to teach me yet another life lesson.

In almost a blazing sprint, well, maybe not that fast because we were weaving our way through the masses, dodging elbows, we were making headway. We heard the faintest muffled sounds from the headsets as we looked at one another. The tour had started. We stopped, trying to find the direction where the signal got stronger. We looked like we were caught in a cage, two steps one way, we decided that was not quite right, so we took three in the other until we identified the direction we needed to head. Before long, we could hear the entire program clear as day, and we turned the corner only to run straight into the thirty plus other members in our group with the same identifiable red headsets.

What a sight! We were short on breath, and my heart was beating out of my chest, like a drum keeping the rhythm of the march. The tension and worry vanquished as a warm breeze swept it off into the distant hills. We had arrived.

My travels had taken me on a road map across Western Europe, from Poland to Ireland, Belgium to Croatia and many places in between. I met a wealth of individuals who were once strangers, but I could now call close friends. I was like a child with eyes wide open seeing the world for the first time with awe and wonderment. I continue to explore and live my life abroad in this way.

I was searching for something at the time, but I didn't know what I would find, until out of the darkness it found me. From dismal lows, where I didn't feel like getting out of bed in the morning, to incredible highs like the time I was standing on the cliff's edge on Croagh Patrick overlooking the tiny islands that dotted the West Coast of Ireland. I finally experienced what it truly meant to live, to put oneself out in the middle of life's beautiful chaos, and to be okay in the midst of change. Yes, I was lost, and I am glad I was. Losing myself in my failed relationship wasn't the end of the world, nor was having hit a stale moment in my career. It was actually exactly what I needed. There was so much more that I had not even figured into my equation. Life is a series of experiences, good and bad, meant to make you wager between the two, to become aware and live up to your innate potential.

I had stopped dreaming, and that had caused me great anxiety. Only to find that it wasn't permanent. Since I was a little girl, I had an amazing imagination and determination to go against the norm, to be different in the face of conformity, to write my own legacy. I thank my ex-boyfriend for the gift he had bestowed upon me. He set me free to dream again, to find my place of peace, to change into the woman I was yet to become.

CHAPTER 1

NOT SO DIFFERENT

"Never regret something that once made you smile."
-Amber Deckers

Exhausted from the day's celebrations, we had just returned home from one of my best friend's going away parties. I had baked an array of confections from salted-caramel brownies to vanilla cupcakes with champagne frosting for the event and was busy tidying up the kitchen, putting away my whisks and pastry supplies when Joshua asked me to sit down on the couch. The day had been remarkable, gathering together with friends and co-workers to wish Morgan, one of our team's bartenders, and her boyfriend Devon a fond farewell as they embarked on a new adventure, exchanging the scorching hot Phoenix summers for blistery cold snow-packed Minneapolis winters.

I had been too caught up in socializing throughout the day to even realize that Josh's demeanor had become very distant. As the evening drew near and guests began to depart, he withdrew from the crowd and sat solemnly at the bar by himself.

I had glanced to where he was sitting to find him deep in thought as I joined the last few girls out on the dance floor. Dancing barefoot on the concrete, a cool breeze ushered in the night as the sun slid below the horizon. We reveled in the last few moments we would all share. Working together over the past three years, we had created lasting memories both on the job and in our private lives. As *Closing Time* started to play over the speakers, we knew this night would end, and we would wish our friends a safe journey north on their new adventure.

When we got back home, I headed straight to the kitchen, no small talk, I just figured Josh was tired. Retiring to the television was an all too familiar pastime. There were no uncharacteristic signs in his behavior that would be cause for alarm or attention, he just seemed preoccupied. That was his typical demeanor either after coming home from work or a night out with friends. He just cozied up with the television remote in hand to unwind to some TV series. It was nothing new. When I looked up from my cleaning, I sensed something was going on, but I wasn't quite certain as to what exactly was weighing on his mind. In the back of my mind, I had a hunch but didn't want to allow myself to let these thoughts cross my mind.

Lying in bed late one night, not but two weeks earlier, he confessed he wanted to break up. He hadn't alluded as to why, but he said he was sure that he didn't see a future with me. I was stunned at this thought and couldn't accept the truth that our relationship was ending, maybe out of fear of being alone or that my plans for the future would, in an instant, cease to exist anymore. Through tears and words of persuasion, I convinced Joshua to give us a chance. Time. That was all we needed. Whatever made him feel like there was no future could be mended if we worked together. That was my co-dependence talking. I was sure I could be the perfect girlfriend if he only could communicate what made him come to these conclusions. I wanted so badly for our relationship to work. I felt like I was drowning, trying to grasp at the threads of a safety rope that just wasn't there. Looking back, I feel pity for the woman I allowed myself to become. I was willing to make sacrifices; I could change my behavior or attitude if only I knew what it was that was upsetting him so much as to want to throw away our five-year relationship.

Naively I thought that this was one of Joshua's phases. We had gone through a handful of breakups and even more passionate make-ups, but something about this felt different. Like a rain cloud just holding out for the right moment to unfurl its torrential showers. Every so often, Joshua would say, "You show potential." I was puzzled by this statement. I always felt that potential meant I wasn't quite good enough. I wasn't the one he wanted to share the rest of his life with, and this was just a strand of string that he wanted me to hold onto until he found just the right woman. Sometimes I even believed Joshua used the word "potential" as motivation. That potential meant if I worked on it, I could one day live up to his expectations. I know this is contorted, that no one who has any amount of self-worth would stand for such demoralizing behavior, but I was weak. No, I was pathetic.

We had lived together twice. The first time I moved out, we took a break in our relationship. We had made a rash decision about moving in together. I had been spending four months in Texas, trying to make a long-distance relationship work. I had moved there to study at the University of Texas in San Antonio and be close to my mother's sister and her family, but my heart gave out. I couldn't stand to be so far away from Josh. I had made the decision to move to the Lone Star State before we met and I didn't change my plans. I was young and ambitious. Now that I met him, I didn't factor the future of our relationship into my plans. I wasn't wholly invested. I didn't actually think it would work out, so I moved to San Antonio. Only after moving, I realized I made a mistake. I loved him. I tried to console my heart and give Texas the opportunity it deserved to fill the void. What wasn't there to love? San Antonio, ranked the seventh-largest city in the United States, houses various facilities of the armed forces.

The vibrant downtown characterized by the beautifully maintained River Walk nestles itself next to The Alamo, a place of historic resistance, and many other 18th century Spanish missions. Texas had real promise. I was offered two restaurant management positions with companies that had plans to expand and grow. I could have established a lucrative career-launching Tex-Mex restaurants in a very up-and-coming culinary scene, while at the same time studying to earn my Bachelor's degree in History. Yet, like a ghost, Joshua lingered in the shadows of my mind. It was one of the only moments in my life, up to that point, that I wondered if I would regret the decisions I made. Not a month after moving out of my aunt's guest bedroom into my own one-bedroom apartment overlooking a rustic timber, where the trees in late autumn were ablaze in auburn and scarlet hues, located in the back of a large gated community, did I decide I wasn't going to stay. I felt like an absolute idiot, foolishly throwing around money and wasting my family's time helping me move back and forth.

Before I left for Texas, Joshua had wanted me to move into his two-story, three-bedroom house, but since he made that offer in late August, he had acquired a roommate who occupied one of his spare bedrooms. I didn't see the addition of another houseguest as a problem and welcomed the idea of living under the roof of a full house alight with energy.

For the better part of a year everything was fine. We celebrated our one-year anniversary with champagne and chocolate-covered strawberries snuggled next to a fireplace in a romantic log cabin sheltered by a canopy of trees along a little creek bed in Sedona, among the red rocks of northern Arizona. He had me pegged. Before we left, he surprised me with an artist easel, paints and the most beautiful diamond tennis bracelet. He never ceased to be a charmer. It was the most magical weekend, wine tastings, spa treatments and an elegant dinner for two at a four-diamond restaurant. I was spoiled. He was thoughtful and endearing on his own terms, but aren't we all.

We loved to travel. I took a short leave of absence, about a month, from my management position at the resort I had been working at before I moved to Texas. They had taken me back with open arms, increased my salary, and even allowed me to take time off. I didn't hesitate to take advantage of these generous conditions making plans to visit France, Spain and Austria. I was turning 23 years old and wanted to celebrate this anniversary under the Eiffel Tower, and I did. I was alone, but it was okay. I treasured the time I had away, especially when things were going well between us. I was confident, self-assured, and this short time apart allowed me to yearn for his embrace. In fact, I wouldn't have to wait long before seeing him again because, at the same time that I took a leave, he too seized the moment to use the sabbatical he had accrued at his job and took a month to visit his family in the Balkans. We met up at the end of the month when our travels were nearing their end, in Vienna, a city of such imperial splendor for a fairytale weekend as though we had stepped back in time to the days of the Hapsburgs. We had planned our trips in such a way that we could both have some time on our own, yet share in a few enchanted memories before we would rendezvous back in the States. When we both returned to Phoenix, we decided to expend our last bits of vacation time for the year and head south-of-the-border to Mexico, spending a warm, refreshing three-day weekend in mid-October in Puerto Peñasco, relaxing on the sundrenched beaches of the Gulf of California.

Traveling was only one of the many passions we shared. It gave us the ability to get away from the stresses of everyday life. After a year of living together, we found the daily grind became too much. Constantly at each other's throat for the most insignificant grievances, we were two strangers inhabiting the same bed. I felt Joshua slipping away to spend time with our roommate and his other guy friends more and more often. That is when I began to get clingy, needy, and frankly, disturbingly insecure. Tensions rose, and arguments became the norm. When Josh called it off and said it was over, I believed him. This was the first of what would be many breakups. I was deeply hurt, but at the same time, I had this inkling, I too missed the freedom of living alone. I was preparing to go to Arizona State University in the fall, and my decision to take Josh up on his offer to move in seemed right at the time but was now unsound. He missed being a bachelor. He was in his late twenties, had a great physique and amazing dark brown eyes. He didn't want to be tied down to any one girl; he wanted to roam. He had an allure that was mysterious. I was his opposite. I was methodical. I had a plan; I always had a plan. But I was happy in our relationship for the most part. Of course, I had my gripes, but we could see that what I wanted was not what he wanted. I felt like I had failed, and with tears welling up in my eyes and slowly running down my cheeks, we went our separate ways.

It took time for the feelings of rejection to subside. I engulfed myself in my studies at ASU trying to finish my third degree. I was enjoying meeting new people and starting to really embrace being single again. That's when Joshua reappeared. It seemed like whenever I put myself back together, he surfaced like he had some sort of radar detection that would signal that I was back on track and exploring the market. For him, this meant there was competition, that someone might actually steal me away and that he would no longer factor into my equation. Even though he may not have wanted a serious relationship with me, he would rather have that than have someone else come into my life, make an impression, and without his consent, I would be gone.

And I, too, held on. Even though I was starting to feel like myself again, going to parties and being social, Joshua still had a place in my heart, and my mind would wander back to thoughts of what could have been. Places we had yet to see and adventures yet to explore. I couldn't just turn my back on the past. I made up the excuse that he got cold feet. That making the commitment to live together was only a mile marker on the road towards marriage, and frankly, he was far from ready to take that path. I remember lying awake at night alone, wondering, longing for the warmth of his body to be near mine. Now Joshua was back and on his best behavior. He was trying to win my affection by joining my friends and me for a night out at a new sushi spot in town.

He started picking me up from campus on the weekend after I'd spent hours in dungeon-like caves, the cold, stark basement of the largest library on campus, researching reels of articles printed during World War I on some ancient computer. Bug-eyed after staring at a screen all morning, we would have lunch on some sunny terrace overlooking Mill Avenue, a busy thoroughfare of lively students and tourists casually meandering in and out of any one of the trendy bars and cafes that dotted the way to school. Our dating was now going well, and we conceded we would give our relationship another chance. I had had boyfriends before, but Joshua was the first one to capture my attention in such a way that I was not only physically attracted to him, but also to his charm, his suave demeanor, that bad-boy attitude. Joshua also had depth, an intellectual ability to lure me in and hold me captive. I was never bored, and that was the key to my devotion.

Nearly three years passed, and we decided to take the next step once again in our relationship, but I was hesitant. I feared that this too would not work out, so much so that my friends jokingly said when they were helping me move my belongings back into Josh's house on a scorching Wednesday afternoon that they would gladly assist me when things went awry. I could have taken this comment offensively, snapping back that I believed in our love, but somewhere deep down I had the notion that what they said would eventually be true. I bit the tip of my tongue and hoped for the best, but had subconsciously prepared for the inevitable.

Slowly, I set down the bowl I was drying and placed the kitchen towel on the chair to dry. I went over to the sofa and sat down with this aching feeling in my stomach that all of a sudden started to reverberate through my body like the onset of the flu, starting from the center and radiating outward. My lower back felt stiff, and my shoulders dropped, heavy like concrete blocks were resting on them. I had a suspicion that what was to come was not what I wanted to hear, that in fact, that unnerving premonition was becoming my reality.

We never had a perfect relationship, and in all actuality, does one even exist? All I know is ours was far from meeting the benchmark for average even at its best. Joshua would come home from work or a night out with the guys very late, sometimes at six or even nine in the morning, without calling or texting me of his whereabouts. Missed calls and voicemails left without return. Some nights he would not even come home at all. It really didn't seem at the time to be too out of the ordinary.

There was a reason for that. Outside of Josh's regular 9-5 job in the office, he found himself waiting tables at the same restaurant where I was bartending on the side to accrue a savings which would afford me the means to travel. I held this job out of pure pleasure for the social engagement. It was relaxed compared to my so-called "big girl" job at the time as a catering sales manager. It allowed me the opportunity to network and was in line with my career. I was working, shaking vodka martinis and pouring big, sumptuous Italian wines for fun, whereas Joshua held this position out of necessity to maintain his habit. It kept him afloat paying bills and financing his vices. Don't get me wrong, this Italian restaurant and wine bar was one of the hottest places in town, so it was lucrative. It gave us a cushion that we would not have had, but it was also this same job that allowed Joshua to keep dealing with what was becoming a compulsion for gambling and drugs. When he didn't come home until the sun crept over the horizon, I just assumed he was at the casino with the guys from the restaurant, many of whom had the same impulses. The world of hospitality has a gritty underbelly for misdeeds, which were oftentimes overlooked as part of the trade.

Over the past eight months since I'd moved into his house, he acted this way with little reverence for my concerns or need for better communication. Joshua was intelligent, he had a successful career in information technologies at a big-name semiconductor manufacturer. At first glance, we seemed like a power couple. I liked classic theatre, going to art museums, and immersing myself in any sort of cultural activity. Josh wasn't as fond of my hobbies, he preferred fishing or playing video games, but he indulged my ambitions and appetite for knowledge on rare occasions. And I made concessions when I found myself at a cocktail party alone or flying solo at some studio opening.

Perhaps, coming from a small town in the Midwest, I didn't know exactly what I was looking for. Of course, growing up, we had our house parties and late-night booze cruises, but it never involved any kind of drug abuse. My first run-in with marijuana was in college when I was going to culinary school, and even that was minimal.

Okay, right away you may ask, why did you stay so long with someone that had these dependencies? They should have been warning signs that would turn off any sensible girl who wanted a healthy relationship. Five years was an awfully long time to tolerate all the negative outcomes that come along with this lifestyle, i.e., lies, disrespect, and secrecy, to name a few. What I once thought was a casual use of marijuana was actually more of irrational use of cocaine. You could quantify it as a remedy for having to put in long hours, that illegal extra pick-me-up or espresso cup that kept him moving like the fury pink energizer bunny that just never stopped. I thought the sleeping until late afternoon was a byproduct of staying out all night at the casino, but it was actually him coming off the high. I still have a hard time discerning drug users unless it is blatantly obvious that hard abuse over time has pillaged their bodies into a disheveled person who barely functions in society.

There's no excuse for my naiveté, I should have known better, but I can't persecute myself for lack of better judgement, I was young, and my heart was involved, intent on convincing my mind of what I should have known was wrong. At times I reminisce about the fruitful side of our relationship, traveling, dining out at first-class eateries and spending time outdoors on the water with the two jet skis we had bought together. We had accumulated quite a repertoire of places we traveled, Austria, England, France, the Netherlands, and Dubai, not to mention the short weekend retreats we often indulged into northern Mexico, Texas, and California. All that aside, he enticed me with his thoughts and was a passionate lover under the covers. He was sensual on his terms, and I resolved to be happy within his fragmented life. These favorable attributes and the history we were building together made me want to easily forgive.

When I started to put the pieces together, it started to make sense. My parents were together in somewhat of a loving relationship, up until I turned thirteen years old. It was then that my parents separated, my mom moved out and got her own apartment. One night when I was there visiting, she asked if I could keep a secret. My mom and I had always been close growing up. She was always the one to take me school clothes shopping, dropping me off at morning volleyball practice and shuttling me to various cheerleading and band competitions. She was always there through the early years of my childhood. My father, on the other hand, was always preoccupied working midnight to noon or noon to midnight shifts at a local printing press factory where he had worked since they got married. He rarely attended any of my games or extracurricular activities. As I entered my adolescent years, my father and my relationship had diminished and was tarnished. I did not know exactly what I was agreeing to when my mother presented this question, but it seemed like an easy answer. Of course, I could keep a secret.

She looked at me and said that she had met someone new. I was in awe, a man? What was she saying, met someone? She was married to my father. How could she meet someone? On one of my mother's many frequent trips to see her sister, my aunt, and a lifelong role model in Arizona, she had met him, her new boyfriend. My aunt was not even aware of this courtship at first. My mother only used her as a cover concealing her affair. For some months, they had been sneaking around having an illustrious romance thousands of miles away from her immediate family and friends. The time I guess had come that she wanted to take the relationship to a new level. She wanted me to meet him with one stipulation; I would never disclose this secret to my father.

That's a huge burden to entrust in a thirteen-year-old girl. I felt conflicted. Yes, on the one hand, I knew it was immoral, but it was my mother who confided this information in me. What was I to say?

I met Rick, a complete opposite of my father in both looks and personality. He was tall, balding, and missing a couple of teeth from his upper gum. My father had grown up working outdoors on motorcycles and classic cars. He was strong, slender, medium height with a full head of chestnut-colored hair. I struggled to see what my mother saw in Rick, but it was not my position to determine her rationale. Very confused by the situation, I really didn't know what to do. I was only thirteen.

Over the course of the next year, my father tried with all his might to convince my mother to move back into our home, to work on herself, to seek counseling. For him, it seemed like my mother was trying to recreate her youth. They had married right out of high school and started a family a year later. She never lived on her own or went to college. Acting out, going to parties, drinking, frolicking around town, and rejecting her family was, in his eyes, her trying to be rebellious. He knew something was wrong but couldn't identify what exactly made my mother throw him away like a scrap a meat to a wild hog. It hadn't dawned on him that over the past couple of years their relationship had been on rocky ground. My mother would go out, not telling my father where she had been. She would come home drunk, reeking of alcohol barely able to stand. He would get enraged and, on occasions, the arguments would get so heated that he would push her down and threaten her. One night I remember crying, hidden under layers of blankets lying on the carpet between my bed and the wall because my father had punched a hole in the kitchen door in a fit of anger.

I kept this secret buried deep inside, eating at my conscience for over a year. One night, after living with this lie I broke down bursting into tears, I told my father about my mother's wrong-doings. I had thought letting go of this weight on my shoulders would be a blessing, somehow it would all work out, but it backfired horribly in my face. My father did not want to believe me, and he called me a liar. My mother felt she had been betrayed. She tormented me with profanity calling me names and saying I was full of deceit. Again, I was fourteen. The vulgarity I endured was not warranted, but I nevertheless took it. These were my parents, what was I to do?

For the next two years, I didn't know where my mother lived. I had no contact. She moved out of the state of Iowa and never tried to contact us. My father still struggled; he didn't want to believe the truth. His marriage had failed. Our already meager relationship suffered. We barely spoke, and if we did, it was in a monotone voice without inflection or tone. We lived under the same roof, but there was no parenting, no love, and no support. We were merely coexisting.

I worked my way through high school. At fourteen years old, I started waiting tables at a local diner where my grandma worked as a veteran waitress. Everyone knew her, and for some reason, had nicknamed her "Flow." I started under my grandmother's supervision, waiting tables for local farmers, truck drivers, and highway patrolmen. The job wasn't hard, and I liked the opportunity I had to meet so many interesting characters. The position also forced me to take responsibility, and I really enjoyed being held accountable for my own well-being and productivity. My first job had a huge impact on the course of study I planned to pursue. From serving customers to trying my hand in the kitchen, I felt like I had a knack for this kind of work. It felt natural, the food and beverage industry. Work was an outlet. It gave me a sense of place and purpose. My co-workers felt like my family when I had a hard time relating to my own.

My mother had used up our college funds, and it was made all too apparent by my father that if I was going to make something of myself, it would be by my own will.

I sat motionless on the sofa as the words no one ever wants to hear came flooding like a tidal wave from Joshua's mouth. He was breaking up with me. He had come to realize somewhere along the way he had fallen out of love. Actually, he had a revelation, he never truly knew if he was "in love" with me. He said I deserved better, that he never felt he could be the man that I expected him to be. I had put unnecessary pressure on him to be the ideal partner. He confessed he always felt he wasn't good enough, and he could no longer go on living this way.

I was in utter shock. My jaw dropped, and I was frozen like a marble statue, unable to move. The past few weeks were rough, but I swore we would prevail. We had been through so many ups and downs, an amusement park ride that simulated a relationship, that I tried not to get worked up on yet another petty squabble.

But this was serious.

My stomach felt like it was full of charcoal, and my mind raced like the fuzzy black and white television screen that likens ants running left to right. I felt light-headed. A whirlwind of emotion raged, tears, mascara running down my face. Emotionally exhausted and vulnerable, it felt like the energy had been drained from every orifice of my being. All I wanted was to be held, to be drawn close, to feel his warmth, but there was nothing left. He was cold and distant. What more could I say?

We sat there in silence.

Crawling under the covers in the guest room that night, I felt my world coming to a crushing halt. What now?

Joshua told me not to stress about moving out right away, that he realized I had an upcoming trip planned to travel abroad with my father to Europe. This was kind in theory, but the vexing unease mounting between us would eventually be too much for me to handle, but I agreed to see if it could work.

Over the years, after I graduated from culinary school, I moved to Phoenix, and with the distance this created, my father and I were able to work on our relationship and communication. I don't think my father ever intended to make me feel unwanted or unloved, but he didn't have the tools to sort out the mess of emotions he was confronted with at the time of my mother's betrayal, and he was even less equipped to cope with his teenage daughter's sensitivities. Once we both matured, we were more prepared to see the scope of the past situation more fully and to understand the frustrations and soiled emotions we both had to deal with. I had sought professional counseling throughout my college career, more to rebuild my own self-worth and ultimately try to instill an understanding that my parent's failed marriage was not my fault. Eventually, we rebuilt our marred relationship one phone call at a time.

My father knew the importance I placed on sharing my passion with him. He had heard me regale in my exploits, working for a Fuller's pub in London near Chiswick on the west end where the brewery was founded in 1845. For the rest of the summer, after I completed my studies in Italy, I was to learn about the hospitality industry in England.

Every time I traveled abroad, my father would be at the other end of the telephone line. Even through our tough times, I always knew I could count on him in the time of need. He lived vicariously through my travels, though it was never his dream. Until one day, he decided, enough was enough, and it was time to see what all the excitement was about.

Joshua breaking up with me did not happen at the most convenient time, not to say anytime is ever convenient for sadness and pain. As I would be away for a month, it didn't make financial sense to take on a new apartment, a new contract agreement. I would be wasting rent on empty walls.

We tried being civil living under the same roof. We sold our mutual belongings. We didn't have a marriage certificate, but I thought to myself this was what divorce would feel like, deciding what was his and mine.

One night while I was at a busy mall shopping for I don't know what, I received a call out of the blue from Holly, Josh's best friend's wife. I picked up the phone. She asked if I heard what had happened to Josh. In a panic, I thought that he had been in a car accident. Even though we were no longer together, he was still constantly on my mind, and I couldn't deny I still had feelings for this man I had shared five years of my life with.

It wasn't that. There was a pause, a moment of silence. "Hello, are you still there? What's going on?" I asked. She goes, "You don't know, really?" I said, "Know what?" The next words to come from the receiver knocked the wind out of me. I couldn't believe what I was hearing on the other end of the line. I sat down not being able to bear the weight of standing; I felt light headed and perplexed.

Joshua had been seeing another woman. In fact, Joshua had the nerve to go behind my back, have an affair, AND get engaged. The knife in the nape of my neck seemed to twist when the voice on the other end of the line said he proposed the day before he broke up with me. I hung my head between my knees sitting in a leather armchair in front of Nordstrom's department store. As Holly said goodbye, I sat there in complete shock and tried to digest everything I was having a hard time grappling to understand. It looked like I was talking to thin air and I was. I was having a full-blown conversation as if I was some deluded junkie on the street. The shoppers passing by turned a quick glance and kept carrying on with their business. My lower lip quivered as the words came out of my mouth, the sham I was living in.

Looking back on it now, that was the defining moment when I knew there was no going back. That was the slap in the face, figuratively of course, that I needed to confront the reality that I had no other choice but to move on and leave the past behind me.

Going home, what was once "our" home, was now "his." I was sick to my stomach. How was I so naive? What did I do to deserve this? All the self-deprecating language I could muster was directed not only at him but also at myself for allowing this to happen. I was crucifying myself for not seeing the signs. Why didn't I leave him when I questioned our ability to withstand the test of time? I should have hit the highway on my own terms and not his. Over the years on any of the given nights, I would lie awake in our bed not knowing when he would return or where he was. What was I thinking? I wanted to scream, and I did. Driving down the street, I yelled at the windshield, thank goodness no one could hear me, they would have thought I lost my mind. I deserved this? I could have filled a whiskey bottle full with the pieces of my broken heart.

I peered into the rearview mirror as I pulled to a stop at a red light on my way. I realized looking at the reflection staring back at me, mascara running down my cheeks, I was no longer an image I recognized. I had lost that zeal, my hunger for life. I was no longer that lighthearted blonde that enjoyed to party and be out in the world creating my own purpose. I had been worn down and had changed so much for a man, for a relationship, that I no longer knew who I was and what I wanted.

I managed to make arrangements to move in with one of my friends temporarily at least until I returned from Europe.

At first, I thought the trip was an inconvenience. What was I doing escaping to Europe when my life was an utter mess, but in all actuality, it was a blessing that changed my life. My original plans were to meet my father in London. He would be flying from Iowa whereas I would arrive earlier than he direct from Phoenix. We would spend ten days together visiting the sights between the United Kingdom and France before he would fly back to the Midwest. After his departure back to the United States, I would remain in Europe on my own for three weeks touring countries that I had not yet had the chance to visit.

The period leading up to my departure was the worst as I was constantly surrounded by reminders of him. The bars we frequented, the movies, even the grocery store. As the departure date circled in red on my calendar neared, I couldn't help but think this day would change the rest of my life or at least I hoped. This opportunity was unlike any other trip I had taken to Europe in the past. I wasn't going there to study, to eat my way through Italy or work in London as I had done many years before. I wasn't on a furlough with my partner madly in love. These were all memories. What tomorrow held in store filled me with anticipation. I had this image of myself on a high board getting ready to dive into the deep.

It may have been easier to have accepted our break up on the terms that we were not for one another, but what struck me as an inexcusable stroke of misfortune was that there was another woman. I wondered what convinced this man to so abruptly get engaged when to my understanding, they had only been dating a few months. I had given five years of my life to Joshua and never got such a commitment. What made her so special? Even though it was his decision, his actions, his morals, I still hated *her*. She knew I existed. She knew my friends. She knew everything, yet she still pursued him. Together I felt, they betrayed me.

This resentment would stay with me for some time. I wasn't happy about keeping these hurtful feelings, but I couldn't seem to relinquish them. It is not a new story, boy meets girl, and they fall in love. Boy has a wandering eye and pursues other interests. So much of the hypocrisy lies in the challenge and the secrecy of the events.

Looking back today, the years were not wasted. I have actually taken from this relationship so many life lessons. I was twenty-one years old when I fell in love with Joshua. Over the course of five years, I grew so much, from a girl into a woman.

People come into and out of our lives for a reason, to teach us something, to impact our lives, to get us from A to B. When their role in our lives is complete they disappear from the scene.

So often we don't realize that every triumph and pitfall we face are learning experiences. They supply us with tools, and these tools are meant to help us navigate life more smoothly. The biggest impact to come from my upbringing was that I tolerated ill-treatment, even treasured it from those closest to me, and I accepted it. I had such a low standard of what amount of love I deserved, that I just collected crumbs from whoever would give me some of their affection.

One night, in particular, stands out where I should have walked away from Joshua because no one in their right mind would have endured such behavior from their partner. As I entered my apartment before we lived together the second time, I heard my mobile ringing from the depths of my purse. I had just gotten off work and wasn't expecting anyone. A gentleman spoke sternly from the other end of the line identifying himself as the chief paramedic responding to a domestic call at my mother's new residence. I knew she had recently moved in with her boyfriend, my grandmother kept me up-to-date on her whereabouts. Our mother/daughter relationship had grown distant, and we hardly spoke, but this night would be different. I was being summoned as my mother's closest next-of-kin to the scene of a suicide. I was in shock. It wasn't my mother but her boyfriend that took his life in front of her. I had no idea what to expect as I parked my Volkswagen behind the ambulance. I had spoken to my grandparents over the phone as I drove to the address the EMT had given me. They were back in Iowa. I didn't mean to alarm them, but I felt it was important to inform them of the situation as well as my aunt and uncle in Texas.

Joshua was also on the list of people I called. I wanted him to meet me at the address, to be there if I needed him and to help me with my mother, who was understandably disoriented and devastated by what just happened. Joshua was out with the guys and made it clear that this was my problem and would not come to my side.

I wasn't comfortable taking my mother home, as she could possibly cause harm to herself or run away in the night. Based upon her past behavior abusing pharmaceuticals, the paramedic suggested another course of action. I conferred with my family over the phone, and the decision was made to request a psychiatric hold to ensure her safety. I followed the ambulance to the regional hospital, where I walked through the stark white hallways to find the nurse in which I had to file the paperwork.

It was nearly four in the morning when I arrived back to my apartment. Sitting down at my desk with a ballpoint pen in hand, I had to complete the petition requesting my mother's hold. It had to be returned in the morning before nine, as I had to be on campus not long after. I felt numb. I couldn't believe how insensitive Josh had been, waving off my problems as an inconvenience he had no mind to deal with. I called him, thinking he had changed his position, that he might come over, and hold me until I fell asleep. It was almost dawn when he answered; it seemed he had just got home from a night of betting at the casino followed by drinks at a local watering hole, then who knows where. From the hoarseness of his voice, it sounded like he was in peculiar form.

I should have known better, what was a modest request blew up to be asking too much. He was not willing to take a five-minute cab ride to be with me. My family melodrama wasn't his, and he wanted to be left out of it. I was in tears of disbelief when I hung up the phone. How could he be so inhuman, insensitive? I wasn't asking him to be at my mother's side, but at mine. In all of our arguments, I had never felt so alone like I was standing in the center of a thunderstorm without cover, exposed and defenseless without a raincoat for comfort and protection from the bombardment of uncontrollable elements.

It would be unfair of me to let all of the burden rest on another's shoulders. As with almost all relationships, when we first started dating, there was a mutual respect, passion, and yearning to embrace one another no matter what. For the first nine months I felt like I could rely on him. We were constantly spending time together, watching movies, going for dinner and drinks. At lunchtime, he would take a break away from the office and show up at the resort I worked at calling me away from my desk to join him at a nearby Mexican cantina for lunch.

Our memories are like reels of film, playing over and over, imagery that can be both uplifting and more often than not disparaging. We analyze what we should or shouldn't have done, but in the end, these mere glimpses back in time are already past.

What I came away with in the end wasn't heartbreak and sadness, though initially, these emotions weighed heavily on my body like unwanted baggage. Over time I relinquished the burden. Setting off on a backpacking adventure across Western Europe was the first of many stages where I experienced a new-found awareness of what a blessing such a failed relationship had to teach.

The lying and cheating wasn't enough to push me forward, it took the extra stab in the back, the engagement, to really make me fully accept that there was no other way to proceed. The universe was telling me that I had learned all I needed to learn from this relationship and that the world was waiting for me to embrace the paintbrush and start a new masterpiece, taking what I could from the past five years, the wisdom I had gained to begin again.

WISDOM 1 TACKLING DEMONS

I was a monster, defeated by the wrath of my own thoughts. All I needed was to allow the words of encouragement my friends supplied to sink in, but I had built a wall, guarding my heart from such sympathies, and dug a hole to crawl in. I was in a downward spiral, and it was not the first time I crawled down this rabbit hole. I blamed myself like I had when my parents' relationship unraveled. I was the punching bag for self-inflicted aggression, and it was getting me nowhere.

It was easy to be the scapegoat, to take the blame, to beat myself up for my shortcomings. Failing to keep a secret, failing to be a better lover, failing to keep relationships intact. I was my number one enemy, but somewhere out of the muck I was wading through I realized I needed to change the conversation in my mind.

I was tolerating a dialogue of self-limiting, critical consciousness, I may have even welcomed it. It wasn't until I became aware of the power these thoughts had over me that I was able to detach from them and fill the void that was left with loving, peaceful affirmations.

Seldom do we accept negative comments from others without rebuke, however, we often accept our own destructive chatter as truth.

Think about it. Only a select group of individuals actually enjoys the company of people whose attitudes are persistently negative. Yet many of us tolerate the demeaning chatter that streams through our own minds. It takes a concerted effort to pay careful attention to thought patterns. When we recognize involuntary thoughts in a nonjudgmental way, we initiate a healing process that will eventually allow us to replace intrusive and distressing banter with positive, encouraging thoughts of compassion.

Occasionally pessimistic or judgmental thoughts will pass through the mind with little to no influence on your contentment, but the unconscious, ongoing negativity that passes like dark storm clouds can have a dampening effect on your mood and your outlook. Becoming aware of your thoughts allows you the opportunity to challenge them and rectify the lies.

I was in a dark place, there's no denying it, but I didn't have to stay there. What I was going through was not so different than what so many others face, what was different was how I responded.

CHAPTER 2

AMERICAN DREAMS

"Change is scary, but you know what is scarier?
Allowing fear to stop you from growing, evolving, and
progressing."
-Mandy Hale

At some point, I believe I thought I had it all. Graduating at the top of my class after having competed in the American Culinary Federation competition in the spring of 2005, I received two degrees in both culinary arts and hospitality management from Kirkwood Community College. That was only the beginning. Leaving the cold Iowa winters behind I moved to Phoenix, Arizona hoping to find a job that would further my hospitality career in a business-driven metropolitan city full of privately owned restaurants, bars and golf resorts. Not long after settling down into the sprawling Phoenix valley, a city continually growing as snowbirds migrate from the north, I went back to school and earned a Bachelor's degree in history from Arizona State University. Burying my nose in historical texts and listening to professors compare the French Revolution to that of the Bolsheviks, I still managed to advance my career as I had anticipated, not only out of personal motivation but also out of financial necessity. Paying tuition wasn't cheap. Rather than take out the dreaded student loan, I held two jobs, worked long hours, and was determined to be the first person in my immediate family to graduate from a four-year institution. Matter of fact, I wasn't quite sure what exactly I would do with the degree, becoming a history teacher in the aftermath of the economic recession was nearly impossible, but somewhere buried deep down was a curiosity to discover the past that had been inspired by my grandmother. To this day, I still wonder to what extent my historical studies will play in my life, and if they will be nothing more than a diploma framed on the wall.

In the true sense of an ideal, I was striving for the "American Dream," wasn't I?

By twenty-three years old, I had managed a privately-owned restaurant in Cedar Rapids, Iowa and through this experience was able to land an entry-level management position at the AAA Four Diamond Arizona Grand Resort overseeing the operations of their fine dining restaurant Latitude 30. This eventually evolved into a horizontal move into catering and sales management and the later promotion making me Assistant General Manager of a three-meal-a-day sports bar and grill on the property. I had a car, a house to call my home, a gray and white four-legged furry feline named Kudo and, what I deemed at the time, a steady relationship.

I was brought up to believe that to achieve this so-called "American Dream" was equivalent to saying that by meeting such and such benchmark, "I have succeeded," or "I am a success." In that sense, I felt like I had failed. My relationship had crumbled, my career had become stagnant and unchallenging, and my self-worth couldn't sink any lower. Maybe my understanding of the "dream" was out-of-date or unrealistic, maybe the American Dream never existed. If that was the case, I thought, then what exactly are we as individuals who inhabit the "land of the free and the home of the brave" trying to achieve in our lives if not some sort of generalized ideal that says, "You have arrived at the prize." And this makes us truly American.

What is the American Dream, if you are like me and believe it still has influence in a capitalist society where we support the entrepreneurial pursuits of the little man and harbor the big business of foreign investment? A nation trying to get ahead, innovating, and transforming itself in order to become better than we once were. To be at the head of the pack and cash in big when the bell rings on Wall Street. What is so wrong with that? Are we not trying to attain some sort of dream, and if so, how to define that which we aspire to achieve? At times I felt like I was holding myself accountable to some notion that everyone was seeking by various means to a similar end.

In his book *The Epic of America*, James Truslow Adams wrote in 1931 that the American dream was "that dream of a land in which life should be better and richer and fuller for everyone, with opportunity for each according to ability or achievement...It is not a dream of motor cars and high wages merely, but a dream of social order in which each man and each woman shall be able to attain to the fullest stature of which they are innately capable, and be recognized by others for what they are, regardless of the fortuitous circumstance of birth or position." (p. 214-215) Adams acknowledges the dream does not or should not lie in materialistic things, motor cars and dividends, but it is the ability to pursue each individuals' rightful truth, or purpose on this earth. Did we stray from this idea?

The authors of the United States' Declaration of Independence held certain truths to be self-evident, "that all are created equal, that they are endowed by their Creator with certain unalienable Rights, that among these are Life, Liberty, and the Pursuit to Happiness." Could this proclamation be considered the basis of the American Dream?

The American Dream is very subjective. A more modern interpretation may say that that the American Dream has become a race, the pursuit of material prosperity, that people work endless hours to acquire bigger homes, fancier cars, opportunity for their families, but in reality have less time to enjoy the seeds they so industriously harvest. I have witnessed the working poor, salvaging what little they have to put a meal on the table or rummaging through dumpsters barely getting by. Working two jobs has become the norm rather than the exception of trying to keep a roof over a family's head in hopes to afford a better future for the next generation. Immigrants can look back on their lives either south of the Rio Grande in Mexico or as a citizen of some other foreign land where they felt deprivation and peril on a level that I hope as an American I will never have to experience. Their eyes see the American Dream from a far different vantage point, treasuring what freedoms they have in the United States, which others often take for granted.

Abandoning my "domesticated belief," as Don Miguel Ruiz calls it, that imbedded truth passed down from my parents, teachers, and other members of society was difficult. For my entire life, I was programmed to believe that material prosperity corresponded with increased happiness. By doing more, earning more, and acquiring more, I would achieve the dream. Yet when I found myself on the cusp of having it all, I felt like something was missing. I had scanned over the fine print but realized I should have paid more attention. **Things do not equate to happiness nor success**. They are just that, things, they collect dust or sit idle in the driveway because you are yet one man and cannot drive two cars at once.

Comparing myself to others and holding myself to a ridiculously high standard was a product of that same conditioning. I unconsciously added another layer of stress to my life by holding dear to my parents' belief system, and falling prey to what I would later learn was ultimately "toxic parenting." I inherited values that seized joy from my life and added a looming cloud of pressure to my every day.

What if we could pick and choose? What if some aspects of the American Dream applied and not others? Coming to the fork in the road deciding whether to turn right or left, I realized the pack on my back was too heavy, and I didn't need so much stuff for the journey. Those things I acquired were actually exhausting, having to maintain car insurance, services, new clothes, when the old ones looked just fine. Minimizing my belongings was just the first step in relinquishing ties to the place I once called home, and the way-of-being that held me captive.

For many, the American Dream could serve as motivation, pushing them forward to achieve more, create more, be more, but for me, it felt like a distraction diverting my energy. Like Facebook, even though I am guilty of this at times, it simply devours our time and energy to receive what in return? I was always comparing myself to others, judging myself, drawing myself down a dark chasm that had an adverse effect. Striving for the American Dream, rather than inspiring happiness, only created more and more discontent with myself and my surroundings. My engrained belief system was acting as a prison, confining me to the tortures of my mind.

I needed to reprogram my ideology, to remove myself from the system for a little while in hopes that seeing and experiencing what the world has to offer outside the borders of the United States would influence these imbedded domesticated beliefs of mine.

I wanted to live abroad, to be my own boss, to have a healthy relationship and start a family. I wanted a career that was creative and inspired, that made a difference in people lives, either helping others find balance in their ever-demanding schedules or having my own bed and breakfast or a quaint little café on some picturesque boulevard where kings and queens once trod.

But in truth, I was an utter mess, the tequila bottle became my best friend, and the worm swimming at the bottom was the therapist telling me nothing more than what I already knew. "I wasn't worth loving." "I was dependent and weak." "I was lost and afraid, sad and lonely." I didn't have it in me to be something great. You don't believe me? Well, the fly on the wall I stared at complacently in a drunken stupor told me I was a raged pile of distressed flesh and bone. Sitting on a ticket to Europe was my only reassurance that this moment would soon pass. Solace waited for me on the other side of the Atlantic. Maybe, I would find my adaptation of the American Dream out there somewhere, on the road between a life I already lived and the one I was searching for.

WISDOM I SHAPED BY THE PAST

I was living by someone else's mile marker for success and not my own. From an early age, much like every child, I was shaped by the influences around me, my parents, teachers, siblings and friends. Growing up in a small farm community, I was raised to have conservative values, be hardworking, and strive for my parents' adaptation of the American Dream. But eventually, I grew up, traveled, and moved to Phoenix, Arizona, where I came in contact with a whole new network of mentors that shaped my world view. I welcomed these new ideas and ways of thinking but still held tight to the ideals set before.

It wasn't until the universe slapped me in the face that I realized my past no longer served to define me and that I was outgrowing the ideology impressed upon me when I was young. These limiting beliefs actually hindered my growth and held me captive. I was still that small-town girl who spread her wings but wasn't quite flying solo. I let others' rules dictate my life, and it wasn't until I started to write my own destiny moving abroad did life actually start to fall into place without so much effort. That's not to say I didn't fall back into old habits and ways of being on occasion, I did.

Even the most vigilant individuals set on changing their behaviors will be surprised by the fact that by nature, we will inherently miss the old patterns as though we would miss a familiar friend. Counterintuitive to change, we humans are creatures of habit, even if those habits are bad. In the face of change, we will often shy away from the unknown out of fear and gravitate back to people and places—and patterns of behavior—that make us feel safe and comfortable.

We may know in our heart of hearts that we need and want change, but it is important to remember habits that we have developed over time are not so easy to break. Having compassion for ourselves as we work through this process can help us stay on course when we feel the impulse to backtrack. In time we will establish new, healthier patterns, and the yearning for the old ones will dissipate.

CHAPTER 3

BAND-AIDS & OPEN WOUNDS

"Would 'sorry' have made any difference? Does it ever? It's just a word. One word against a thousand actions."
-Sarah Ockler

Sitting at the arrivals gate with my feet up on the edge of my suitcase and nose only slightly dug into a self-help book, I was warily watching for a familiar face to come walking through the doors from the baggage claim of the international arrivals terminal. Arriving via Air Canada into London's Heathrow International Airport three hours before the scheduled arrival of my father, I watched minute by mind-numbing minute pass as lovers embraced, families united, and business professionals slowly made their way out into the crowd. A little over a month had passed since Joshua and I split, but such a short amount of time was not nearly enough to heel the gaping wound such an upset created. I sulked and brooded knowing full well, life would not stay this way, but I was unable to find the resolve to move on. Considering I was an emotional mess, my father still agreed to come. He had sat quietly on the receiving end of so many distressed phone calls listening to muffled sniffles and harried questions why? He still didn't know quite what to say or how to handle his daughter in such a sensitive situation, but he was learning.

He too had gone through many disappointing breakups leaving him disheveled with those unrelenting questions why, so he could empathize with my pain. Not so certain he knew exactly what he was getting himself into, I had to respect the man for trying.

Catching a later flight from Iowa through Chicago O'Hare, this slight delay between our arrivals was intentional. I was not only dealing with inexorable sadness, but I was also nervous. It was my father's first time outside of the continental United States, well, if you count the Bahamas, maybe it was his second, but he never possessed a passport in his life. He was fifty years old. London wasn't some Podunk, hick town in the middle of nowhere that he was flying into with one terminal and one exit door. London Heathrow, a labyrinth of terminals, exit doors, and lifts, one could feel like a mouse in a maze trying to navigate the twist and turns and overhead signs leading to one of many ways out. I did not want my father to end up like a rodent running around in circles chasing his tail, so I took precautions and arrived early. I planned ahead and emailed a detailed list of instructions from departing the jet bridge to customs. He would retrieve his luggage at the baggage claim, walk through the final duty free shop and out into the arrivals hall where he would be greeted by me, a little weary from my own travels, but no less inclined to fetch a hug. After our rendezvous, we would make our way down to the trains and on into the city.

I had convinced my father back in January that this year was the year that any unexpected expenses could wait. After he had been in a motorcycle accident in 2007, where he was rear-ended on a gravel road, thrown from his bike and his leg was absolutely gutted (the skin had peeled back from the flesh) he had changed. The utterly painful ordeal and near-death experience made him see the world a little differently. Having been told he would never walk without a cane, he mustered the strength and surmounted the odds. Not that I would call the accident a blessing, it was far from that, but it did cause my father to have a revelation. He realized he was not fully living. Before this, he was stuck in auto-pilot saving for retirement, putting dividends in his 401k, and trying to manage risk at all costs. How would your life savings serve you if you were six feet underground? It would merely facilitate the enjoyment of the next generation, and I, nor my brother, aspired to such an exuberant inheritance.

I knew something inside him had changed when he agreed to jump out of a perfectly good airplane at 13,000 feet strapped tandem to a beautiful woman with over 1,500 jumps to her name. He would never have done something so death-defying before his motorcycle accident. It just wasn't in his nature to tango with life until he felt the rush and exhilaration plummeting toward earth in a total free fall. The experience made him want to venture further outside his comfort zone.

My motivation was selfish in some regard. Yes, of course, I wanted him to expand his horizons, to see the great wonders and hopefully meet some amazing people along the way, but for me, it was a personal vendetta. I wanted to show him all that I had accomplished, maybe we wouldn't make it to Italy to show him where I had studied, but I could take him where I had worked in London in the summer of 2004. I could tour him around one of my favorite cities in the world, from the Imperial War Museum to the Tate Modern, from the West End Theatres to St. James Park. I never had parents that were interested in my grades or wanted to see my report card at the end of the term. They were too transfixed on their own melodrama to have concern for my schooling or my personal achievements. I never got the pat on the back or "good job," but similarly, I never got reprimanded either. They just weren't interested nor involved, and I wanted that to change. I still sought that validation wanting to know that I had made them proud. I didn't think I would ever hear those words from my mother, that she was pleased with me, but my father was different. My grandma always told me that dad was proud of his children, but he never addressed me with those words of adoration. Was he shy, or didn't he know how to express himself? I was not quite sure.

There was one hiccup though, the timing was awful! In January, it would have all been different. The weather would have been frigid getting dark in the middle of the afternoon, but I would have at least been a joy to be around. In the present situation, I was far from being the best travel companion.

Moping around, my mind was preoccupied rehashing the events of the recent past. I tried to play tour guide to the best of my abilities pointing out sites from Big Ben to the Tower of London, but I got frustrated easily, unaccustomed to having such a novice traveler following my every move. He was always two steps behind me not wanting to lose sight, for fear he might lose his way. I didn't understand this behavior. My patience was short, and I lashed out when I didn't mean to. It wasn't my dad's fault, I should have been more patient and understanding, but I didn't have it in me to take him by the hand and show him the ropes, I just didn't have the energy. I needed him to be inquisitive, to want to learn and discover, but London just wasn't his "cup of tea."

I should have known better, a man born and raised in the country would only be comfortable in similar surroundings, and it wasn't until we reached Normandy, France that I saw some stress ease off his shoulders.

Bayeux, a medieval town four miles from the English Channel would be our base for exploring the region, from a Battle Bus Tour of the Beaches of Normandy to paying our respects to the troops that lost their lives in Europe during WWII at the American cemetery. My father was overwhelmed by the heralding stories of paratroopers being dropped behind enemy lines and the Army Rangers assault on Pointe du Hoc scaling the cliffs to disarm the battery on D-Day.

The highlight of our tour through Northern France was an excursion, no, a pilgrimage to Mont Saint Michel in the midst of gusting wind and spitting rain. I only say pilgrimage, because this majestic Benedictine Abbey perched on a small rocky island between Brittany and Normandy had topped my bucket list for some time. Every year I made it my goal to one day visit this magnificent architectural wonder that still inspires awe. I was excited to share such a once-in-a-lifetime experience with my father, and I believed he truly enjoyed it as well.

Sitting in a Parisian café later in the day, my father revealed that he didn't really like the French capital. Dirty, packed with tourists he didn't feel at home like he had in the Normand countryside with its horse pastures and apple orchards. Yes, he was enamored by the years of history in which his feet tread, from the likes of Napoleon Bonaparte to King Louise the 16th, but as for feeling at ease, the language, the congestion, the culture left him wanting his little house on the hill. Ten days was quite enough for him to be away, and he was all too forthcoming with letting me know.

Disgruntled and impatient to leave, my father and I were on each other's last nerve, ready to snap at any time.

I didn't foresee that my father would be so discontented with Paris, a city so enchanted with historical sophistication, memorable architecture, and vibrant art and fashion that has spanned centuries. It is hard not to be completely infatuated by the romanticism in it all.

From the small closet-sized hotel rooms sleeping on a twin bed with a single duvet to a bland, unexciting breakfast the hotel offered at an exorbitant price, I could understand his disdain, but it went a little farther than that. Europe wasn't the United States. I had grown to accept the differences and actually found humor rather than frustration in many of the variances. It is something you accept, like waiting for service or having to constantly ask for a check. If you were looking for American style hospitality, then it is best to choose any one of the fifty states as your preferred holiday destination.

Paris has its charm, but I believe my father had built a wall. Culture shock had set in, and he refused to see any beauty whatsoever. I became frustrated and even resentful of his behavior. I wanted to believe he could overcome this, that we could enjoy the last few days we had together, but tension continued to escalate. One morning, after forgoing the so-called, "Continental Breakfast," a croissant with jams, sliced deli meats and cheeses and flavored fruit yogurts at a cost of nearly twenty euros, we headed to a café shop around the corner. He, of course, had to wait for me to finish getting ready, which annoyed him. Hostillity mounting, he didn't have the confidence to venture out and find the shop himself as I had suggested, telling him I would shortly follow. In this case, he was reliant upon me to navigate the streets, and this made him feel helpless.

After being prodded to hurry up and get ready, we were out the door. Stopping in a commercial bakery that offered very little in way of homemade delicacies, I relented. He was hungry. Yet, I will confess one of my biggest pet peeves while traveling is dining at or consuming something that is processed or fast food. Whether a croissant from Paul's or a salad from Starbuck's, they lack the heart that you get from a local patisserie or family-owned, one-of-a-kind brasserie. Convenience was the name of the game. Since waiting god forbid a half-hour longer for me to be ready, my father had become ravished and was apt to eat any drab packaged croissant with ham and cheese or perfectly round donut. I know this makes me sound uppity, and when it comes to food, I will confess, I am a little prissy. I know what I like, what I will or will not put into my body and this wasn't it. My father filled his tray, and I grabbed a cappuccino. What can I say?

He was frustrated with me and I with him. My depressed mood was weighing on us both. Whenever we stopped for a break, I would pull out my journal, and he would be left to watch people passing by, a favorite pastime of many, but not him. I wasn't engaging. I didn't want to hear one more complaint about being confined to the city and his overwhelming anticipation to go home. After lunch, we were looking for the metro and something he said set me off.

It was like a tidal wave of built-up resentment had broken the dam and rushed from a space within. I couldn't put a plug in it. What I had to say needed to be released for it had been mounting for years. Things I had repressed since childhood started to spew out of nowhere, a geyser of anger and pain. I didn't mean to unleash on my father who didn't expect such fury from such a tiny body, but he was a convenient one-man audience. He was family. It's always easier to verbally thrash the ones closest to you than to have a mental breakdown and complete unraveling with a total stranger or friend, because you believe no matter how hurtful or mean you are to them, they will continue to love and accept you.

What came out wasn't even about Joshua, the root of my sadness, though the feelings of rejection caused other repressed thoughts from my past to gurgle to the surface. I thought I had come to terms with my parents' divorce by rekindling my friendship with my father and having a civil relationship with my mother, but I was horribly mistaken. Out of the depths of a very dark place in my soul, I felt I was deserving of an apology and, by deserving, I mean demanding an apology. I still resented my parents for the hurt they caused me during the most influential years of my life. The separation and ultimate divorce scarred me. I felt unable to create and hold fast to meaningful relationships because I was never led by example. I was placing blame on my father that it was his fault that Joshua and I were no longer together. I wasn't able to allow myself to get close to people because I only felt rejection in a time I was trying to find my place in this world. I felt victimized by the divorce. I was made to be the bad guy. I never understood what a healthy relationship looked like. I was never brought up to believe in love. As children, we were hardly shown affection, even today, hugs are rare and likely uncomfortable when given. I was mad that in a sea of people, I had never felt lonelier.

Standing at the stairway leading down into the metro, I was in tears pleading for an apology. It was the culmination of it all. A failed relationship, the feelings of being lost, my father's discontent, the fact that I had the mental space to brood over events from my past and somehow irrationally tie them into my present situation. I knew it was unfair of me, but in the present state I was in, there was no convincing me otherwise. I knew my parents' divorce did not cause Joshua and me to break up, but I was searching for a scapegoat. Anything that I could leverage to free me from the convictions in my mind. I was trying to justify that it was because I was brought up in a house torn of love, that I too was incapable of feeling and in turn giving love to another.

"You are supposed to be the parent. Apologize. Stop acting like we are equal because we are not. My mother has apologized for her behavior, never once have I heard a word of regret spoken from you." My father stood there, speechless. I had talked about the divorce with less emotional attachment before when we were in London, and maybe he had given the subject some thought because, after a short pause, he was forthcoming with an authentic apology that struck me that he too had buried hurt and anguish deep inside. "I was doing the best I could with what I had. I was trying to keep our family together at all cost not concerned with the traumatic impact it would have on you. I was depressed, I could hardly keep myself from falling to pieces, let alone be a good parent. I overlooked the damage done...I know it wasn't your fault and you were right to tell the truth." Relief. The grown man who stood in front of me looked defeated. It was still early in the day, but he was haggard. I didn't mean to beat such sentiments from him, but if I never confronted the conversation, we would never have been able to put the past fully behind us and move on with our lives.

The admission of guilt was not the primary motive for my outburst, but I didn't really have any control over myself. Thank God it was my father because any other rational human being would have thought I had gone too far.

We were quiet for the rest of the afternoon taking the metro to the Château Rouge stop and climbing the stairs up to the Sacré-Cœur Basillica located in Montmartre. Perched on a hilltop the Roman Catholic Church constructed in a Romanesque style stands triumphantly overlooking a web of city streets below. Still trailing steps behind, my father could not get over his fear of getting lost, but after the conversation I put him through, I decided to leave him alone for a little while. Why harass him anymore, what good would it do? I already hurt his feelings, and this might be the only thing he takes away from the whole experience of being abroad. I hoped not, but I couldn't say for sure.

Unable to leave the city limits for the rolling hills of the French countryside, I did what I could to make the last day we had together somewhat enjoyable. Sunny skies with a few trace clouds and a gentle breeze, the day was ideal for canvassing the city on foot, and that is what we did. Instead of being cooped up in any of Paris' marvelous museums, which would have been an utter bore for my father, we just meandered for hours through the late afternoon and early evening through quaint neighborhood parks where grandparents watched their grandchildren play. It may not have been the freshest country air, but for Paris, it would do. Away from the bustling crowds and the noisy city streets, we walked in uninterrupted reflection.

This day would soon be behind us. My father would take from his travels what he would. My only hope was that I didn't inflict a lasting negative impression of Europe as a whole by my childish, mean-tempered conduct that could ultimately mar his entire memory of our time together, never to return.

No matter how rotten I felt, I was glad my father was there. He was the sounding block I needed to get all of the ugliness off my chest. As much as I asked for an apology, I should have given one in return. I was a nightmare to be around, but I know at some point, whether he wanted to talk about it or not, he had been in my shoes and could empathize with the state of agony I was in. He didn't expect remorse, and at the time, I wasn't giving it.

We would leave it on these terms.

An apology given, an experience had. He was on his way back to the lush green pastures and place he called home. Back to his friends, back to his routine, back to everything that made him feel safe and secure. I was out to discover, to face my demons, to feel uncomfortable and at times, lonely. I was on an adventure to come into my own and to take a journey that was only about to begin.

WISDOM 1 CO-DEPENDENT BEHAVIOR

Constantly I was trying to please other people and seek their approval, but why? Looking back, having played an integral part to the unraveling of my parents' marriage at a very young age was traumatic, but I only brushed the experience under the rug. I left the feelings of hurt and longing buried doormat for years. As a teenager growing up in my father's house, I was constantly searching for his approval and never received praise. I found myself overachieving, juggling multiple jobs, fulfilling the role as the caretaker in my mother's absence, and settling for unhealthy relationships because I desired to feel acceptance from those around me. I was scared of being alone and abandoned so much that I would do anything for love. These symptoms I am describing are characteristic of someone who is codependent, and by definition, it's a loss of self because you're too busy taking care of others or worried about what they think, feel and want.

I carried all of these toxic attributes and unresolved issues with me into my adult relationships, even the one I had with my father. I was repeating traits that were unsatisfying, limiting and self-deprecating because they were familiar, and that was what I thought was normal. I wasn't shown what a healthy relationship was and ultimately didn't feel I deserved one.

The world needs giving, loving, compassionate and empathic people but not at the expense of sacrifice. You too need to receive love, kindness and compassion in return. I eventually opened my eyes to my codependency. Accepting the cycle of giving AND receiving took time because I had conformed to a one-sided relationship for far too long with not only Joshua but with my parents. By accepting my codependent behavior without questioning it, I was hindering myself from pursuing my true purpose and path in life. Ambivalent to my actions and despite my best intentions, I was also depriving those individuals that I cared for of the lessons they needed to learn and grow.

The truth is I was causing myself unnecessary suffering and needed to help myself out of this cycle of destruction.

CHAPTER 4

PARTY FOR ONE

"The farther I travel, the closer I am to myself."
-Andrew McCarthy

Why am I drawn to the bad boy types? I know they will only break my heart.

A tour guide, really? What do I have with tour guides, why are they so damn attractive? Is it their funny jokes or their ridiculous egos that I am drawn to the most? Maybe it is their intellect…they have to be knowledgeable about the script they sell, right? They're good salesmen, that's it! That's why my knees melt every time Kyle walks in the room. He wasn't the first tour guide I would have a harmless crush on, but it would be the last, as these sorts of relations were in the end unrewarding. My first infatuation with a tour guide was nothing more than a magical weekend in Austria years ago. I was drawn to the man because of his thick Australian accent and bright crystal blue eyes, like those of a Siberian husky. His gaze was mesmerizing. His name was Adam, and the weekend we shared together left me wanting more. Of course it did! We had a spontaneous spark of passion that faded as I boarded the train to my next destination. I was 22 at the time, and it was irrational to think that I could just disregard my plans, my obligations for nothing more than romantic desire.

The butterflies I felt fluttering around inside my stomach were a good sign. For over a month and a half, I felt numb, both emotionally and physically, like standing in a walk-in freezer without noticing the cold. I was ambivalent to feeling. I started to wonder if I would ever get out of this funk I was living in. The first ten days I spent with my father were draining. I had wanted to be a good daughter and travel companion, but my heart just wasn't in it.

England and France were now behind me, and my father had made his trans-Atlantic quest home to his little ranch style house snug on top a hill overlooking a sea of cornfields. My first stop on the train from Paris was technically Brussels, which only served as a layover, allowing me to catch the next train north to Bruges. A charming little hamlet, crisscrossed by picturesque canals and Gothic architecture, welcomed me back in time to an era of horse-drawn buggies and ladies in extravagant petticoats. History aside, if I wasn't careful walking through the old city center I could have been trampled by the clattering hooves drawn by guides narrating Bruges's economic importance as a center of trade as early as the 12th and 13th centuries to eager tourists with their eyes wide open relishing the city's timeless beauty.

It wasn't that I was looking for a relationship, oh no. I hadn't even come to grips with the last one. Every day I felt like I was pummeled by rain clouds continuously looming overhead, showering gloomy thoughts, and a dismal outlook on a very nearsighted future. I had only come to Bruges and more importantly to Belgium for two reasons, the beer, which I consider to be the golden nectar of the gods and the collection of Flemish Primitive artworks created by a wide range of Renaissance and Baroque masters in the region. The lord only knows I was in no condition to be a good partner or even a good friend for that matter. How could I contribute to someone else's life when I couldn't even hold mine together? I was still sulking in misery and jealousy. I couldn't erase the thoughts of Joshua and his now fiancé out of my mind. Entertaining the thought of a one-night stand could help facilitate a faster recovery from the nightmare I was putting myself through. The only obstacle in my way was to find the right candidate to encourage me to change my stance. That is where Kyle entered the scene.

He drew my attention straight away, maybe it was the fact that I could recognize his East Coast American accent from the crowd. It didn't sound like mine, a flat accent from the Mid-West, and it surely wasn't a laid-back California accent. I had lived on the west coast long enough to differentiate, but it was distinguishable from the plethora of other languages buzzing about the hostel's reception. There was something mysterious about him. Checking into my room for the weekend, I noticed a sign-up sheet posted on the wall for a beer tasting that very same evening. Wanting to see if I was interested in attending the tasting, Kyle approached me. Assuring me it was an event not to be missed, he vouched for the facilitator saying he was charming and hilarious.

Why not, I was in Belgium? The land of the holy nectar. Belgian beer was one of the primary motivations behind my interest in the country. Well, initially, I guess. I knew there was more this tiny nation had to offer, but it was far from my mind. Where did this fascination come from, you might ask? A woman who likes beer, awesome! Maybe a decade ago this statement would be far from the norm, but becoming a beer connoisseur or a beer snob is in fashion. I was turned on by artisan beer in the States. Microbreweries were emerging on what seemed like every street corner, but coming from years working in the restaurant industry and staying abreast on global trends, I knew even better beers existed abroad. Belgium, nestled in the heart of Northern Europe's so-called "beer belt," is a region characterized by a relatively moderate climate and fertile soil particularly favorable to growing cereals that are highly distinctive in character and taste. Adding the presence of fresh mineral water to the equation led to the expansive range of quality beers produced by small family-run breweries, monasteries known for their Trappist beers and big conglomerations.

I was enticed by Kyle's confidence and demeanor regarding a subject I too felt very passionate about. I was intrigued, and if it meant maybe seeing him again, why not? Sign me up!

Before going anywhere though I had to do my laundry. After two weeks of living out of a suitcase, my clothes could almost stand on their own. The feeling of putting on the same sweater three days in a row was repulsive, and it was time to feel like a clean, well put together woman again, not just some drifter traipsing across the continent. I freshened myself up in the locker room style bathrooms, a communal facility commonly found in youth hostels, making them affordable. No luxuries here, just the bare essentials. It wasn't like I was getting ready for some fine dining dinner; it was just a jovial beer tasting in the comfortable backpacker's bar conveniently located on the ground floor of the hostel building.

I wandered downstairs where people congregated around the bar and near the television getting ready to watch the inaugural match of the Euro Cup action that was getting underway in Poland. Other patrons not so enthralled by the tournament spilled out onto the street in general merriment. The sky was clear, and temperature mild, which I would soon come to find was rarely the case in Belgium, not well adored for its weather.

I was a little early. Walking up to the bar, I noticed Kyle sitting near the end of the counter in the corner of the room. He was eating dinner with the staff. I didn't know if he worked here or what exactly his deal was, but he seemed to be the person to know as everyone hovered around him trying to make conversation. The place started to get crowded as I elbowed my way through the mass of individuals queued to get a drink. The friendly staff seemed knowledgeable. They had a lot of beers available mostly in bottle, some I had seen before and even had been able to find back in the States, but some labels were new. The bartender made small talk as he hurried back and forth, helping other patrons. I thumbed through the menu and asked for one of my favorites before hopping onto a nearby bar stool.

As the time for the beer tasting approached, Kyle got up from the bar and started to round up the participants almost like a cattle call. Of course, Kyle, the guy giving the presentation, was entertaining because he talked about himself the entire time. How vain?! I fell for it like a giddy little school girl who had a crush on the boy next door.

We packed into the corner of the adjoining restaurant, a small space dimly lit with dark wood paneling, which felt like a cigar room tucked away in an old rural English pub. The tables were set up with small tasting glasses and on display were five thoughtfully selected beers we would soon be tasting. My mouth salivated.

The best part about staying in a youth hostel is that you never know who you are going to meet. I was surrounded by a few Italians, some Aussies, a Brit and a group of American guys. I would come to find out later these guys were soldiers in the US military stationed in Brussels and were only in Bruges to show some friends from Tucson around for the long Memorial Day weekend.

Caution, a warning should be given to those just tuning into the beer scene in Belgium. If you are not used to high alcohol content beers, do not drink them like your favorite pilsner back home. Belgian beer is a work of art. It is crafted from centuries of tradition in brewing. The final product is typically a higher alcohol content beer that is balanced by a variety of hops and malt, adding character and intrigue to every sip.

Kyle lived up to his presumptions; he was very amusing, combining details about Belgian beer with comedic satire. For example, he poured every beer that we tasted but the last one, Duvel. The name itself literally means "The Devil," with 8.5% alcohol content it powers a jarring punch with a light body, vibrant carbonation and a unique effervescence that is very desirable, yet again should come with a warning label. One leads to two and before you know it you are not acting quite yourself. Not sure if Kyle was speaking the truth or coming up with his own rendition of an old wives' tale. He said traditionally, because of the obscure effect this beer had on patrons, bartenders from the late nineteenth century until today refuse to pour the beer in its own specific glass etched with the letter "D" into the bottom.

Witty and charming, mixed with rude vulgarity and unconventional tactics, there was no wonder he made a successful career as a tour guide for fun-loving backpackers. He offered a package that was not your traditional run of the mill city tour, and that is testament to his own character. He would start every tour by giving a disclaimer that he would not try to be politically correct and that there was no human resource department for complaints. If you couldn't handle his dark, uncouth humor, that was the queue to take leave and find a more refined tour. There were plenty in a city driven by tourism. Cunning and obnoxious at times, he won his way into your heart.

How did he get to Bruges from living in downtown New York City, I wondered? Of course, Europe had its appeal. I, for one, would jump on the opportunity if it were presented to stay on, but how did he make it happen? Not too dissimilar to other tragic fairytales, he fell in love with Bruges, well not exactly. He was traveling for three months, typically what backpackers do. For any given amount of time, they set out to learn, discover, and just be out in the world with no responsibility and no one, in particular, to answer to.

Bruges suited Kyle. When he decided to stay on at a small youth hostel, he started to work at their reception while boarding in one of the rooms, making it affordable to live on an indefinite basis. Wait, did I forget to mention there was a girl, not very original, right? There is always a girl. Boy meets girl, they fall in love. Boy decides to give up all the comforts of home to be with her, and so the story goes. Working at the youth hostel, there was no shortage of entertainment, and for the first year or two, the days just seemed to wash together. A passionate love affair in one of the most picturesque cities in Northern Europe.

As with most stories of this nature, the fairy tale came to a crushing end. He had invested his time and given up almost everything he had back home. Deciding against the odds, he stayed. He started small, growing his business from beer tastings, adding day tours and bar crawls. He had a bright future, and the market was right.

Over the course of the evening's events, I was coaxed by my fellow Americans to join them on Kyle's bar crawl. What was I thinking? As I was nearing my dreaded thirties, okay, I was 26, but I thought that this spirited behavior catered more to the 18, 19-year old's, and early twenty-some's among us. But hey, the American guys were also my age if not older. If they could keep up with the youngsters, so could I. Against my better judgement of the looming headache and hangover that could potentially follow after a night of drinking Belgian beers and shots of Genever, Belgium's national spirit from which gin evolved, I consented. I still had a party girl buried deep inside, waiting to get back out on the field and play some games.

Hitting my threshold before we even left the hostel, I tucked myself in with the guys and followed the crowd. If they consumed shots, I consumed water. At least until I got a trace of my bearings back. Over the past month and a half, I had used alcohol as a crutch helping me deal with Joshua and my break up, and I was trying to break the habit of drinking myself into a disheveled state that was less than becoming. I vowed that I wouldn't turn into the hot mess so often typical of recent high school grads or college students out to have a good time no matter what the cost. Time and time again, staying in youth hostels on my travels, I saw friends and acquaintances having to usher in their drunk cohorts after a night of boozing.

Traveling on my own had made me wise. Having no one to look out for you, there was no telling the trouble you could get in if you let your guard down. It is not that I learned this from experience, I never had a blackout moment where my drink was laced or ended up in a rave. That was not my style. I liked risk, but not unnecessary risk. I liked to have a good time, yes, I have fallen into the strong arms of handsome strangers on a few occasions, but I had my wits about me to make sure it was a decision I was comfortable with. Making friends was relatively easy, but it wasn't like you had an established rapport, you could never know what they would act like after a few beers or a bottle of wine. So, I always tried to make a point to watch out for my best interest.

When I could feel the effects of the first round of beers wearing off, I decided I could hang with the guys. As we approached our last bar for the night, my silly flirtatious side got the better of me. Who was this girl, I thought? It was as though I was having an out of body experience. It had been five years since I had last been on the dating scene, and I felt like times had changed, I had changed. I was young and foolish back then, and now I was out-of-date. If I were to be a contender vying for Kyle's attention, my tactics needed to be reformed.

Now I was older, more mature, well at least I thought so, but my behavior begged to differ. I played and poked fun, like a school girl picking on her first love on the jungle gym. I had no reference to how this worked, dating, it had been so long. I guess it wasn't that bad, as he took the bait.

We walked back towards the hostel that night holding hands. I could hardly control my nervousness. A spark of interest, a feeling I hadn't had in a very long time. I had thought my heart had been broken past the point of repair. We started to kiss, just standing there on the street corner. I was wrapped in his arms, and under the glow of the street lights overhead, he pulled me in close, slipping his hands into my pants pockets. His gentle lips caressed mine. What was I doing? I wanted to rip his clothes off, to have my way with him. Passions high, there were two ways this night could end.

My rational sense slowly came back to me as we took a breath from our heated make-out session. What got into me? I hardly knew this man who stood in front of me, and it seemed like I was about ready to jump into the sheets with him. This was a whole new level for me. I know the weeks leading up to this were a dark haze, depression, bats of anxious emotions and drinking, lots of drinking. I had only wanted to increase the detachment from emotion, to feel utterly numb. Now this?! I was standing here on a street corner exchanging passionate kisses with almost a complete stranger. Really, who I was I becoming? I was never the floozy, the bimbo or just the bubbly blond looking for attention. That wasn't me. I was fun, just never the center of attention, but somehow, I fit the role under the star-studded sky.

Gaining my composure, I rashly interrupted him with some comments that I should go now and it was getting late. Without hesitation, I started to turn and go. He reached for my arm, as my hand slipped through his, "When can I see you again?" "Really?" I thought to myself. My confidence had hit an all-time low in the weeks preceding this, so it came out of the blue that I was actually worth seeing again. I told him I would be around the next couple of days and that hopefully, we would cross paths again. Without another word, I turned abruptly 180 degrees and walked briskly into the shadows of the night.

I left him with his head spinning. I guess the mere fact that I nearly broke off in a sprint in the opposite direction after being so intimate moments before made him a bit curious. He later told me that it had never happened to him before, where the girl just took off like the boogie man confronted her. It was not my nature to be so rude, but this was foreign territory where I wanted to tread lightly. The whole idea of dating again left me unsettled. After Joshua, I wasn't sure if I could trust again.

What was I thinking?! I was getting a bit ahead of myself. Who said anything about a relationship? We had merely kissed and nothing more. I was playing out these fantasies in my head. I wondered when I would see him again. In the midst of so many very dark days, I had the faintest glimmer of light.

This love affair wouldn't just last the weekend. We spent all of Kyle's free time going out to dinner in restaurants along the many canals, having beers, sharing stories, and getting to know one another better on a personal level. I spent the next few nights curled up under the covers of his bed wrapped in his arms, our naked bodies exhausted after hours of making love. It was so nice to wake up to a now-familiar face that kissed my eyelids before whispering "good morning." My roommates at the hostel had to wonder where I was at night as my bed was empty and undisturbed in the morning. My heart felt at peace, such an unusual feeling, one I had not felt in so long.

Surely though my time in Bruges would come to an end. I had planned the next leg of my trip, and I had places to be I couldn't put off. I couldn't just cancel my flight to Poland on a whim. I couldn't just squander my time waiting for him to finish his work to be with me. I would again be living for a man, and that was a function I did not want a repeat performance of. I had lost myself once, never again.

As much as it pained me, I said my goodbyes on the platform as the train to Brussels approached. I had arranged catching up with those crazy American guys from the bar crawl. They were soldiers in the Army and Navy. They had all served in Afghanistan together. They reminded me of my brother, a soldier in the United States

Army. He too served in the Middle East right after he graduated basic training in the wake of the September 11 attacks. For whatever reason, I felt a gentle familiarity. They were gracious and easy to talk to just like my brother. I felt like if I needed protection, they would step in and thwart off danger. The ones that were stationed in Brussels worked for the US Army Garrison and acted as support staff at NATO. How wonderful this random meeting. I felt a connection to home that was unexpected. They had invited me to come to Brussels to show me around before I had to catch my flight to Warsaw.

It pained me to look back, seeing Kyle standing on the platform that slowly faded into the distance as the train picked up speed, but I had to move on. I had a summer of experience to look forward to, and this was only the first step of many across the map leading the way back to myself. If I gave into the first relationship that presented itself, I would be doing myself a disservice. What would I really learn? I would be hopping from one man to the next and never resettle back into my own skin. I would always be associated with another, and that was far from what I intended when I embarked on this journey.

Did I have feelings for Kyle? Yes, but I couldn't tell if they were only fleeting. I couldn't stand the risk that if I were to stay, I would be diminishing my growth, so I ventured on, leaving the book open-ended.

WISDOM I BALANCING THE HEART AND MIND

Listening to that little voice inside your mind is sometimes hard to do. Against the intentions of a fiery, passionate heart that wants to coast on an emotional high, the rational sense of the mind has to take hold for the greater good.

We have all been there, torn by the internal conflict between the heart and the mind. It is evident that the mind is theoretical, vastly learned by experience, and is only looking out for your best interest, while the heart knows no limits of irrationality. Some may argue, it isn't even meant to be tamed. When left on its own, the brain has to monitor the heart, to step in at the right moment and bring you back to earth and a sound rationale.

If you were left to the will of the heart, you'd probably allow yourself to give in to every fleeting desire that could potentially leave you broken and hurt more often than not. It is a tight rope we walk on, balancing the desires of the heart and the prudence of the mind.

The heart will bring you joy in the most disagreeable conditions, and the mind will help you walk through seemingly pleasant situations, which are an illusion to reality. Knowing which to follow is as subjective as it is situational. When it is time to make a decision, it is never going to be the heart or the mind on the sour end of the losing stick; it will just be you, losing your sense of self.

Remind yourself to be careful as you tread down a new path. Finding balance between the powers of the mind and the heart can be done by listening to that little voice inside that speaks the truth, your intuition. It may not be what you want to hear, and sometimes you may have to defy it to chart a new path, but you will have to weigh the options wisely and with prudence. Life-altering decisions are not made overnight. A thought, yes, a motivation, but it is important to give this idea due diligence before seeing it through to fruition to make sure it is what is meant to guide you forward. Be honest and true with yourself about what is leading you toward a healthy future and what may direct you astray.

CHAPTER 5

LEARNING TO LOVE

"Love and kindness are never wasted. They always make a difference. They bless the ones who receive them, and they bless you, the giver."
-Barbara de Angelis

Łukasz was at the airport waiting. I couldn't find him at the arrivals gate at first. He was talking to a group of police officers who were trying to give him a parking ticket. He had arrived early just in case my flight was ahead of schedule, which caused him this slight hiccup. I was on time, and he had overstayed his welcome in the short-term curbside parking. After he smoothed things out with the police, he quickly came to my rescue.

Unsure of who to expect in the arrival's terminal, I was pleasantly surprised. You see someone's profile online, and you're never quite sure who will actually show up in person. Will their picture be the face that waits in front of you? This was the first time I would try out this idea of crashing on a stranger's couch. I had heard about it before. A good friend of mine from Australia had told me he had used this organization of travelers to find accommodation in Munich during Oktoberfest. He said it worked remarkably well, with a set of safety valves such as feedback and ratings to control misconduct and abuse.

David, a young, charismatic marketing professional who was traveling for six months around Western Europe was able to find a host, a young woman who gave him the keys to her apartment, no questions asked. She didn't have to give up her entire apartment; typically, that is not the premise. The idea is focused on sharing the experience, meeting travelers and getting to know them and vice versa. In this case, David's host stayed over at her boyfriend's place giving David her entire home during one of the biggest beer festivals in the world. While even the most frugal youth hostels were selling bunk beds for 100 euros per night, my friend was staying for free in the comforts of someone else's home. The only exchange was the possibility of sharing one's time and the value of cultural interaction.

"Couch surfing" wasn't a new idea; it has been around for some time. The idea is to create a community of individuals who cherish the more modern nomadic life, leaving the comforts of their jobs and every day responsibilities to be out in the world anywhere from two weeks to two years. I am a couch surfer and, by this, I mean I am a member with a profile. According to the site, these nomadic individuals comprise one of the world's largest travel groups, a volunteer-based network of travelers who want to break away from the subscribed normal routine of everyday existence and share real-life experiences with complete strangers. The main objective is centered on creating personal relationships and engaging in activities with people from around the globe in your own back yard or out on the road.

Okay, it may not be everyone's idealized way of travel. I think the first time I told my father about the concept he feared for my safety, yet he knew he couldn't stop me. I assure you. There are protective measures in place to help guarantee there is no foul play when choosing to crash a couch or host a surfer, and I told my father this trying to suppress his worry. For me, this program has only ever been rewarding, and I have accumulated a handful of experiences from staying with Łukasz in Poland to crashing on couches in Ireland, Switzerland, Italy and Croatia. I even hosted a young traveler from Nice, France when I returned to the United States, but enough about that for now.

Łukasz could not have made more of a positive first impression. He took the time out of his day to personally pick me up at the airport when he could easily have just given me the directions via public transport to his apartment on the outer edge of the city. In a country where I would have been completely lost because of my complete lack of comprehension of the Polish language, Łukasz came to my aid. His generous hospitality made me feel right at home.

It wasn't long before we were off exploring the city. Łukasz, like many Poles I have met since, is very proud of his heritage. Well-educated about his country's turbulent past, he was the perfect tour guide. Considering my passion for history, with a main focus on the greater twentieth century, he indulged my inner geek. I am a self-proclaimed nerd when it comes to history. I get a high from acquiring new information or hearing a different perspective to facts I already know. In the end, history is subjective and, if you are open-minded, it can be absolutely fascinating comparing particulars and opinions.

Growing up in the United States we covered what led up to World War I, the aftermath, and the defining moments of World War II, but my history lessons as a child were nowhere as in-depth or captivating as hearing them from someone firsthand. Łukasz may not have been personally engaged nor alive during the Warsaw Uprising or lived through the majority of the Soviet era and the Iron Curtain, but he had relatives and acquaintances who were. Speaking with Łukasz and having my feet on the ground seeing the Communist architecture, visiting museums and landmarks of where public killings took place during the Nazi occupation gave me a deeper appreciation and understanding of their unsettled history and their perseverance in the face of evil and misfortune.

As we walked through the Old Town in Warsaw looking out over the Vistula River, my mind began to wander, reanalyzing how I got into the funk I was in. Kyle had been a lovely distraction, but momentary, fleeting like rain in the desert. He was like a pain reliever helping me cope, but at any given moment, I would see a shred of light that would lift me from the hell I was living in only to fall back into the festering thoughts of my mind. A battle raged within me, ever wanting to put this ordeal behind me, but not knowing how. Łukasz was perceptive about the turmoil I was in, maybe it was because he grew up with a younger sister, which made him more sympathetic and understanding than other men. He asked questions trying to get me out of my destructive thoughts and back to the present. He asked about where I was from and where I was going, the redundant ice breakers I would answer over and over again as the weeks turned into months out on the road. It was hard to deny what was going on in my life; it was all too apparent from my appearance that I wasn't a carefree, happy-go-lucky hippy trekking across Europe living out her childhood fantasies. Rather Europe was a drawn-out therapy session that had not yet started to work its magic. Awareness was the first step in the process. I would come to realize my response was always the same,

I kept reliving the past by telling people about my horrible break up. Maybe I wanted sympathy. Maybe I was playing the role of the victim, I didn't deserve what had happened. Or maybe, in fact, I wanted to suffer more. I was the one causing the drama. I wasn't good enough; if I were good enough to be loved, I would still be in a relationship. By continuing to recount my miseries, I allowed myself to wallow in my sorrow and distance myself further. This pattern had to change.

For the next couple of days, I would have a lot of time to myself. Łukasz worked for a large financial firm downtown, and his days in the office were long. His sister who lived with him in his tiny one-bedroom apartment with a pull-out couch, which served as the "second" bedroom, was at school all day and would only be back home for dinner on most nights I would be staying with them. This left me alone with my thoughts. There wasn't anyone to amuse me. I had to start facing my self-destructive habits or let them ruin me entirely.

I awoke on the sleeper sofa with the sun shining through the slits in the curtains and the smell of coffee wafting into the room from the kitchen just around the corner. Łukasz was already up and moving about getting ready for work. The air mattress, his makeshift bed for the night, had already been tucked out of the way. His steps were quiet not wanting to disturb my slumber, and I relished this as he carefully set the table right in front of me, not even noticing I was awake.

After all, the walking around downtown and going for a peaceful stroll through the Łazienki Park the day before, my body was weary. I wanted to stay curled up warm under the covers for a few more hours closing myself off to the world and finding solitude in my dreams, but that wouldn't make me a very gracious guest.

Stretching my legs and getting acquainted with my new surroundings, I was greeted by a table of local cured meats and aged cheeses accompanied by the most succulent fresh strawberries which Łukasz had bought from the farmer's stand on the street corner in front of the apartment complex. This was a welcomed surprise considering my typical breakfast back home in the States consisted of drip coffee and multi-grain toast with butter and jam. I didn't put much thought into breakfast since I taught yoga most mornings; the lighter the meal, the better I felt, but there was something remarkable about this spread of delicious local fare. It brought back memories of summers long past when I would spend my days at my grandmother's house in the Iowa countryside. Grandma and I would wake up very early on a specially selected day in June when the strawberries were at the peak of harvest. We would go out to the strawberry farm, a swatch of land with acres and acres of strawberry patches as far as the eye could see. On bended knees, we would pick baskets full of plump strawberries, crimson jewels that would explode with the sweet flavor of summer. My grandma would spend the succeeding days by the stove stewing the succulent gems into the most amazing mouthwatering jam, only to be stored in the cellar for those cold winter nights when we would spread the jam over soft, fresh-baked bread. Somehow, I would convince my grandma to save some fresh berries to be devoured with angel food cake and fresh whipped cream. This, the reward from our exploits.

After breakfast, my hosts were out the door and off to work and school. I was left with a set of keys and all the time in the world to ready myself for the day's activity. I decided I would try to get out of my head by practicing some yoga, so I rolled my mat out in the middle of the small living space and turned the music on.

I had been carrying my navy-blue yoga mat with me slung over my shoulder since I started my travels. Nearly a month had passed, and only now I decided to pull it out and put it into use. I would wonder later on why I actually brought it in the first place. I guess I had good intentions, but in the end, it would cause me more hassle getting on and off trains, maneuvering through crowds of pedestrians and collecting dust than it was worth. In the end, I guess it served as a good reminder to ground myself and enjoy the moment.

Time was on my side, of course, I could rush through my travels from A to B, but what was the point? It would be a superficial experience, like one of those 10-day cruises through the Mediterranean docking in a major European city every day. What do you really take away from the experience? The bright and shiny highlights, the major tourist attractions, but you never really get to feel the beating heart of the city because you are in a hurry to get somewhere else.

For me, I looked at this opportunity as a once in a lifetime experience. So many people race off after college graduation into a career, start a family, and before they know it, half of their lives have passed them by. Americans especially devote themselves to long hours in the workplace with little to no holidays in comparison to their European counterparts. Retirement serves as a benchmark when many finally start living out their lives more fully, but not me. Long ago, I had made a pact with myself. I would not wait until my retirement to see the world's wonders. I would not be that old lady with the cane or walker struggling to climb the mountain or visit the Louvre for example, when youth was on my side now.

After working hard through college and into my twenties, I had a cushion saved up in anticipation that I would need it someday, and that day was now. I estimated I would need approximately $1500 a month to be comfortable, to see the sights I wanted, pay for internal flights in Europe, rail, accommodation and meals. It sounds like very little, and it was, but you don't have to have a fortune to travel. You do have to have a solid understanding that necessities come first and sometimes less is more. Traveling with only what you need for basic comfort will allow you to easily navigate city to city, country to country with little to no hassle with security, maneuvering yourself on and off trains and climbing up flights of stairs. I wasn't looking for luxury and was quite satisfied with staying in youth hostels, the occasional bed and breakfast or budget hotel which on average would cost anywhere from $30-$40 a night if you did your research and planned shortly in advance. I was always looking at least one week ahead to my next destination, jumping on various travel websites to scout out the best deals. New boutique hostels were popping up all over Europe from Prague to London and everywhere in between. Sharing a room with anywhere from four to sixteen roommates may sound a bit overwhelming at first, but many hostels have the futuristic compartment beds called Pods that look like a cubicle where the bed is encased by three walls, and a canvas can be drawn giving you privacy from the other guests.

As a solo traveler, it is not only affordability that influence guests' choices, but these places provide the means in which to easily socialize and engage in interests while visiting a city that make them pleasant alternatives to more traditional hotels. In planning my exploits abroad, I set some guidelines when it came to activities, balancing free guided tours and entrance fares to museums with more costly wine tours, river rafting or day trips. I had this mindset that I didn't have to relish in all my dreams and ambitions at once. I would be back; it was never a "once-in-a-lifetime" circumstance. If I sought to do everything to which I aspired, what more would I have to look forward to later in life? My policy was simply this. If I was intrigued, I would go for it, but if I felt the opportunity could wait, I put it on my to-do list for another moment in time.

If accommodation was the biggest expense, transportation would come in second. There are many factors that would affect costs here. Traveling by train in some countries is quite affordable, and in others, it is quite the opposite, but offers for students and various passes catering to the avid traveler make traversing the European continent more accessible.

Nothing is more quintessential to travel as food. Culture is experienced not only through various forms of art, music, language, religion and design, but it is reflected in the cuisine of each individual nation or region. The table serves to break down barriers that may exist politically or spiritually and ushers in an experience that warms the soul. Nourishment, one of the most basic human needs, is a form of communication sharing the knowledge of the land and its people. I remember going to Rome around Easter time. I have a friend who is Italian from the small town Rivolio close to Turin in the North, where his work took him to Rome for 12 years. When I met him, he was no longer a resident Roman, but he was more than happy to share his wealth of expertise and contacts which only an insider could extend. The first evening he called ahead from Barcelona where he was now living to make a reservation at what I would come to find as a very discreet restaurant in the Jewish quarter. One door, surrounded by a string of holiday lights that flashed red and white, if you were not careful, you would blindly walk past the entrance on the way to one of the ancient romantic bridges crossing the languid Tiber River flowing through the heart of the city. The kitchen offered three seating times, and they were all fully booked. My friend managed to reserve a table for me tucked in the corner of a brightly lit dining room that was not fancy, but more informal, dawned with old newspaper clippings framed on the wall recounting the restaurant's upstanding history and some small works of art that could have been reproductions of Renaissance paintings. Traditional strong wood four post tables were small in dimension, making it easy for the family who ran the little establishment to usher back and forth catering to the various sized reservations. The food wasn't complex, but the ingredients were of the finest quality, delicately prepared to make the most finicky patron a fan.

Of course, dining out can pinch the pocketbook if you are not managing your finances properly. Often at midday or for a late afternoon snack that could serve as both lunch and dinner, I would find a local shop for cured meats like prosciutto, artisan cheese, my favorites Pecorino Romano or Asiago Pressato and seasonal fruit. Taking a regional wine or cider to some sunny spot overlooking antiquated ruins or artistic wonders served as an intimate backdrop for the most heavenly picnic.

Affording myself time without stress or worry about finances was a well-deserved blessing for all my hard work. I wasn't rushing off to buy a house or put my money toward a life insurance policy. That would have been conservative behavior, maybe what was expected of me, but it wouldn't have created a very exciting story to tell.

What next? How could I take the best advantage of this venture, this investment in my well-being?

First, I needed to get one thing established, where did I go wrong? Why did I lose myself? When did I let go of my own wants and dreams and start living for a man? I had to take back my life, and the first step of many would-be identifying what inspired me. What moved me to want more, and by saying more, what exactly was "more"? Where did my happiness lie? It was becoming clear, after arriving in Poland, I started to become open to my feelings, and the answers would surely come.

I had been manipulated for so long into believing that I was the root to all our problems as a couple. I was insecure, having to call him late at night when he didn't come home from working at the restaurant, only to be forwarded to his voicemail. I would come to find he was at the casino all night, sleeping the weekends away. Our time together was minimal.

Having big ambitions always served as motivation. I wanted to own a bed and breakfast in Italy one day, yet for some reason, I could never see Josh in my dreams. I tried to paint the picture in my mind foretelling the future. Telling myself he would straighten out, get his life organized, seek support for his gambling addiction, but it didn't happen, at least not while I was in the picture.

Establishing strict guidelines and boundaries was something new to me, and in order for me to move on, it was essential that I implement them. For so long, I had given into other people's needs and wants, not only Joshua but my parents, friends, co-workers and bosses. I would try my best to make everyone happy first and foremost before considering my own time, my own interests. I felt like I was always trying to win the affection of others, their approval. This was something I was doing to myself, but others could capitalize upon it. For instance, I was given a promotion from Assistant Restaurant Manager to become the temporary General Manager of a large restaurant and event space for three months during the peak tourist season only to have that title removed at the end of the summer, and my salary dropped significantly to where it had been. The management of the property didn't hire a new general manager when this temporary promotion ended. They just assumed I would fulfill the role until I had enough. They had taken a gamble. I had to fulfill a contract that outlined the lesser salary for one year. When I was "demoted," six months still remained. They ran the risk and used my management skills until I resigned at the end of my contract. I hadn't been fairly compensated.

Łukasz couldn't have been more of a perfect example of the new kind of friend I was trying to find. His genuine, sincere personality and kindness was what I needed to experience. He was traveled. We shared many of the same interests, such as art, history and the wonder of the outdoors. We could relate on many levels from talking about the Soviet occupation, which I had studied for a semester at ASU, to finding the best pierogi, or Polish "ravioli," in town. Believing a city alone couldn't make you fall in love but the people that you find yourself surrounded by made all the difference if it was to feel like home or not.

I would continually attract new friends into my sphere over the coming months that would fit the same profile, compassionate hearts that had no other intention than to offer friendship, support and their time.

This was the hurdle. Taking the lessons and putting them into practice. Not dwelling on the past but actively engaging it, learning from it in order to make 1 changes in my life. This would be a daunting task. M on meant having to pull buried emotions out from behind the shadows and back into the light. I was going in the right direction, but I wasn't out of the woods just quite yet.

WISDOM 1 THE POWER OF REFLECTION

What if I offered you a tool that could change your life in a positive way, change your reality, create more bliss, and help you achieve everything that you aspire? Would you buy what I am selling?

I know we all have busy lives, and it is easy to get lost in the moment, the day, the week or even the month. Some people are so driven, they can speed through an entire year without pause.

Prioritizing self-reflection takes a personal commitment. It requires us to make time for profound thought, analysis and consideration. To say we don't have time is a meager excuse. If it is important to create change, schedule time to write in your journal or sit in silence as though it were a top appointment or professional conference that would support the personal development of your life because it will.

What does reflection look like? It is time that you set aside to sit in quiet thought, asking yourself questions that make you get in touch with your core values, intentions, actions, relationships and ways of being. Writing down these thoughts can be a great way to organize those things that make you feel grounded, on track with your goals and work through those things that may give cause for unease. Outline areas that are out of flux and need to be realigned or amended. Looking for generalizations, patterns, tendencies and underlying principles can be extremely beneficial. These overarching takeaways can be applied to our lives and help us see where inconsistencies lie. By becoming mindful and aware of the musings of the mind and getting them out on paper, we can find more clarity and peace in the everyday.

It may sound self-absorbed to some, but if I am not fully committed to my own well-being through conscious reflection, I am absolutely no good to others.

CHAPTER 6

GENTLE KINDNESS

"I am not what has happened to me, I am what I chose to become."
-Carl Jung

Traveling on your own pushes you to be more extroverted. Flying solo sounds great but can only last so long. At some point, the need for social interaction will be so great that even the most introverted person will require outside stimulation. The solitude of a quiet hotel room only offers an excuse to stay inside your own bubble, to confine yourself from unique interactions that so often take place in the unlikeliest of places.

Somehow over the years, Adam and I stayed in touch. A tour guide from Australia whom I had been involved with on a previous trip to Europe had made me wonder what might have been if only I had not gotten on that damn train.

Seventy-two hours in Vienna was all it took to fall head over heels for a man that wasn't my boyfriend. I knew better, I was still dating Joshua, but playful flirting led us to Adam's apartment, sipping a nightcap of

Austrian schnapps on his terrace under the stars. I was conscious of my decision when I slipped off my black stilettos and flung my silk skirt over the lampshade. For three weeks, Joshua had not responded to my calls and emails, and though my promiscuity could be questioned, I felt like we were on the fringe of calling it off. I had moved to Texas and took off to Europe in the wake of the transition, and the long-distance relationship was not boding well.

The next morning Adam had grabbed my pants' back pocket as I walked out the portico from the interior courtyard and onto the sidewalk to go back to my hostel. He pulled me in close as he slipped me his number and kissed my hand as though chivalry was still alive and well. I was off to Salzburg at noon, but he would join me later in the evening as he had to return the bikes he used for his tours to a friend's garage.

An unexpected affair ushered in so many ludicrous questions. I was not wholly committed to Texas; I had left Phoenix rather reluctantly, not knowing where I was meant to be when life wheeled me this curveball. A handsome man that crawled into bed beside me caressed my body and pulled me into himself. His powerful hands made me feel safe as he spoke to me softly. His season had ended, and he was off to holiday in Majorca. This unexpected meeting had his head spinning and heart drawn. If I were to stay, there would be no hesitation on his part as to whether he would abandon his plans to be with me, to follow me to my next destination. I just needed to say the word.

The train departed at two. After sleeping, wrapped in each other's arms until noon, I knew I wasn't ready. As Adam carried my luggage, I pondered the thought. What if I were to stay? I was only twenty-three. I had wanted change—that was the whole premise behind moving to Texas. I didn't think Phoenix offered me the room I needed to grow, but now there was a very enchanting offer from a gorgeous man. Was I up for it? Somewhere deep inside, I wanted to say absolutely. Throwing caution to the wind would have made for a heralding romance, and my life would have been wildly different, had I not stepped foot on the train headed for Munich. Alone, I stored my suitcase and fell into my seat as the train slowly chugged down the tracks. I could see a crossroads in my life left undecided as the figure of a beautiful man faded into the distance.

He had moved onto a serious relationship that had taken some rough turns and left him with his heart in his hands. Hugging one another at the arrivals gate in the Dublin International Airport we both needed this weekend away. Five years had passed, and time had affected us. It was like meeting an old friend for the first time all over again. Filling in the missing blanks by being overly inquisitive, I was nervous honestly. We had exchanged casual emails over the years that had passed, but seeing him there in person, feeling his warm embrace felt familiar, yet distant at the same time.

Having flown to Ireland three days earlier from Poland, it was the third country I would cross on my roadmap of Europe. I was getting used to being on my own, though I still battled with the chaos in my head.

I wanted to put Joshua behind me, but he crept into the dark spaces of my mind and festered there like a virus needing to run its course. I wanted a quick fix, a magic potion to make it all go away, but the best I could muster was an invitation. A little birdie dropped the envelope on Adam's computer screen when he gave the reins of his now thriving bike and wine tour company to his assistant and galloped in on a white jet plane.

Picking up the keys from the rental car agent, our plans were to set out towards Galway on the western coast of Ireland and drive up the coast to Sligo, a popular surfer's village. The rain was relentless; it was Ireland, what else could you expect? Storm clouds plaguing the skies, yet, the torrent of rain did not dampen our adventures. Taking coastal roads, following the route north, we saw nature unfold before our eyes, waves crashing on the rocks, edging our way from one small fisherman's enclave to the next as we drove inland. From the valleys, you could look up at the steep hills carpeted in lush green vegetation and see majestic waterfalls tucked into the ridges of ancient passageways. The experience was surreal.

Picking up our friendship from where we had left it was puzzling, yet awing. We were both on the mend from broken hearts and quite forthright about it, sharing every detail, without fear of judgment or rejection. Though we had been intimate before, neither one of us was in a state to let our inhibitions run wild until we had a few drinks in. Our conversation was loose; we talked about the passion we shared once upon a time, which led us nowhere. It was like we had lived another life, yet all roads led back to this juncture: lovers and friends.

We slept in the same bed, cuddling and talking under the covers, yet nothing happened. It was anticlimactic. There was a point at which Adam had leaned in to kiss me, but I was naïve and thought nothing of it, waving the gesture off like a fly. I was nothing like the girl that had slipped off her skirt and fallen into his arms back in Vienna, and I would argue he was not the same man.

We were both hardened by love. He didn't have the same air of confidence and domineering spirit that had me mesmerized me before. He was reactive, not the alpha showman I once knew. Of course, that was okay, but the spark that once blazed bright was a smoldering match that had an end.

The day before we had to return to Dublin, we stopped off in Westport, a small town halfway down the coast to Galway. The sun started to peek out from behind the rain clouds, burning off the cold, bleak blanket of grey. Looking at a map, we had acquired from a local tourist office, we slowly approached the entrance to a nature park reserve which the man behind the counter had circled in red. On closer observation, now having read the plaque at the information booth leading to the entrance, this was a spiritual pilgrimage site dedicated to the patron saint of Ireland, Croagh Patrick. Ireland's holiest mountain became a popular religious destination drawing locals and tourist from near and far because it was said that Saint Patrick completed a forty-day Lenten ritual of fasting and penance overlooking Clew Bay in County Mayo.

Let's just establish that the hike, or pilgrimage to be more exact, is not meant for the faint at heart. With peaks reaching 762 meters (2500 feet) above sea level, it is not so much the elevation that offers the challenge, but the shards of fragmented rock that make an unsteady base for gaining footing. Trekking carefully to the top, the mount offers rewarding views of the 365 islands that dot the waters in the bay below.

There was just enough break in the weather to take the hiking boots from the trunk and tackle the nearly four-hour trail up and back. At first, I thought I would ascend the mountain without any problem. Being a yoga instructor, I thought I was fit. Walking 15 kilometers a day, I had been very active the past few weeks, but fit may have been a misevaluation.

As I began to ascend, I very quickly started to get short of breath. My legs were in motion, but I was having a hard time pushing forward. My mind badgered me with its notoriously insulting self-talk I hadn't yet mastered the art of muffling. "Dummy, you are not trained for this, what were you thinking, silly girl?" "What did you sign yourself up for?" My brain was racing faster than my footsteps, running down the reasons why I would embarrass myself trying to conquer this feat. Finally catching up to Adam on the first landing, I tried to catch my breath. As the elevation rose, the air began to thin, and breathing became more difficult, making it hard for me to form sentences. Adam was on pace, trekking along steadily ahead, unaware that I struggled falling significantly behind.

Noticing after a couple of minutes had passed, I was dragging behind, he backtracked to where I rested against a boulder and asked if I was okay. The mental dialogue playing in my head was telling me I would never make it, that I should quit now and not waste time. "Get out while you still can!" I told myself.

Out of nowhere, Adam's gentle words of encouragement lifted me back to my feet. I never knew him to be the motivating type, but who was I kidding, we had never spent this much time together. How would I really know his type? Before, I had made horrible assumptions that he was the bad boy type only looking to score and was frankly found wrong in my judgement. This time I had made no presumptions and was pleasantly surprised. When my strength wavered, he stepped into give me the extra push I needed. Cheering me onward and upward, he truly wanted me to succeed. How absurd that I couldn't rally the strength on my own, that I wasn't able to convince myself I could do it.

After Adam's fervent coaxing, I heard that little voice inside change its tune. I began reassuring myself that I could conquer this, convincing myself that each step would get me closer to my goal, and eventually, I rose to the top. Others joined me. A group of Englishmen had been right beside me through the last stretch singing the *Eye of the Tiger* on their ascent, and this made me laugh. As silly as it sounds, I felt like Rocky Balboa after running to the top of the stairs raising my arms to the sky.

From that moment on, I had more patience with myself. The self-deprecation was debilitating, and Adam helped me realize this. Against the odds, I could achieve the impossible if only I believed I could.

Adam would be one of many friends who would guide me along my journey. Sweeping in like a loyal knight, he helped me to see my old ways of thinking no longer served a purpose in my life.

Sometimes we cannot take on the world on our own, and often we forget this. Venturing off on this weekend getaway served to remind me that there are people there to lean on for support, that through the toughest trials, are there to help me prevail.

Many of my closest friends came into my life through similar experiences. I have been blessed by many rare meetings that blossomed into resilient friendships. Most of these individuals I met on my travels. When I think about them, I remember the fond place in my heart they keep. They hold this special place because they saw the real me and accepted me even at my worst when I had nothing to offer in return for their friendship. When I think back, these friends all came into my life when I least expected them to, when I wasn't looking.

WISDOM 1 ACCEPTING HELP

I didn't realize I needed help. I thought I could handle the burden of pain I was going through on my own, with passing time, but I was sorely mistaken. The downward spiral spun out of control, and I was living in my own worst nightmare. Fortunately, this unflattering side of me was overlooked by friendship. Adam offered a compassionate heart that would show me the ultimate kindness, empathizing with the turmoil I was putting myself through.

We have all been there. On the opposite side of the conversation when we hear some rendition of "it's not you, it's me." Words with such strength, they could wrench the fibers of our hearts and cast us off like trash in the gutter. A wretched feeling of unworthiness makes you want to crawl under the covers and wallow in self-pity. There really is no reason to mask your emotions, to put on a happy face when all you want to do is cry. It is okay to be miserable, to be vulnerable, to feel angry and rejected. It is not weakness; it's honesty. We shouldn't feel ashamed for expressing our true selves, or allowing the weight of life show when times are rough.

Adam and I were going through the same anguish together, although he could tell I was fighting some merciless fiends. Twelve years my senior, his last relationship was not his first heartbreak and, nor was mine, but he had acquired more wisdom and strength that he shared freely and openly. He offered me the gift of a kind heart and sturdy shoulders to lean on.

That's it. Adam was real. We were friends, and that's what true friends do for one another. Ask for help or receive it graciously when a kind soul extends his hand. Often our egos get in the way and are blinded by our own hurt and are too proud to accept or ask for help from those people we surround ourselves with, but we should. That's what being human is all about. Recognizing that we are all equal, that wisdom is best shared, and a gentle word or warm embrace can do wonders to help a broken heart and restore confidence. We need this assurance in the midst of unrest. Everything will turn out alright.

Open your heart and allow yourself to be surprised. When the covers are drawn back, and you open yourself up to receiving this amazing gift, you will change.

Led by example, Adam had more faith in me than I had in myself at the time. By being receptive to this, I was able to change the hurtful patterns I was tormenting myself with. I could embrace a new beginning, leaving my depressing conduct in the wake. I received his help and found strength.

CHAPTER 7

TRUSTING STRANGERS

**"A journey is best measured in friends,
rather than miles."
-Tim Cahill**

Reservations aside, I signed up for a sailing adventure off the coast of Croatia with a complete stranger. It was just him and the boat. For all I knew, I could have been sailing out to some remote place in the middle of nowhere. The sea has a great ability to have its way, leaving us desolate and alone floating at the will of the wind and the waves. A dire scenario, I could have been tied up to an anchor and dropped to the sea bed, and no one would have been the wiser. I had made one last-minute phone call to my father back in Iowa telling him about my great plans with excitement and zeal, not wanting to cause him undue stress and worry that what I was about to embark on would not be normally advised for young women traveling alone.

I guess the thought of running off to the sun-drenched skies and crystal blue waters along the Dalmatian Coast with a complete stranger sounded spontaneous, exciting, full of wonder, but there was a flip side to the coin.

Sipping a cup of coffee, I had burrowed my way to a corner seat on a small terrace in a crowded little café overlooking the bustling streets full of tourists in the restored Old Town in Warsaw. I was in the heart of the city, making plans for the next leg of my trip as I stared into my computer. I was looking at accommodation. After my successful stay in Warsaw with Łukasz I thought I would try staying with another stranger, but unfortunately, I wasn't able to find anyone that had an available room or a couch for the dates I would be in Krakow. So, without hesitation, I booked a youth hostel in the middle of all the tourist attractions. Ideally located down one of the narrow streets leading away from the Cloth Hall on the main market square, the hostel, from what it looked like on the map was close to the Wawel Castle, nestled up on a hill overlooking the Vistula River. I had never been to Krakow before, a city virtually unscathed by World War II, unlike the rest of Poland, had much of its pre-war charm left intact.

I made the slow-moving three-and-a-half-hour train trip south to Krakow from Warsaw, a city that ranked high on my bucket list for no other reason than intrigue. Playing the role as the capital of the General Government, and having the close proximity to Auschwitz, the Nazi death camp, it was a wonder how it came away unscarred by the brutalities of war.

Staying in Warsaw had been great, a big metropolitan capital, busy with business but vastly different from Krakow. Once the imperial capital, Krakow offered culture and allure that the cold, stark office buildings and Soviet architecture still ever-present in Warsaw from the Cold War could not compete with. Setting aside a whole week for this leg of my journey was a must, there was so much information to absorb.

By now, I had a routine. When I arrived to a new city, I wanted to get acquainted with my surroundings, and that typically started at the local tourist office by picking up a city map and exploring the various options for tours and places of interest. Krakow was full of activity offering day trips to Auschwitz to the east and salt mines to the south. There was even a tour company that took those wanting to be out in nature to Zakopane, a winter wonderland in Poland near the Slovakian border. Even though it was a cold-weather destination nestled at the foot of the Tatra Mountains, the southern city offered splendid hikes and breathtaking scenery to the outdoor enthusiast.

I wanted to immerse myself in Poland's history associated with the region and joined two walking tours of the city. One showcased Krakow as the once-beloved Royal City dating back to the 7th century. The other tour took on a much more solemn tone as we uncovered the remnants of what was left from the communist era, Nowa Huta, one of the 18 districts or subsects of Krakow. The neighborhood, said to be the most inhabited areas in Krakow today, characterized by its communist block architecture, is able to accommodate numerous families in cheap, no-frills housing. Constructed of concrete panels, *Panelaks*, the term given to these long unremarkable structures, rose to over twenty stories high and had been criticized for their unsophisticated design, second-rate materials, low-quality construction and obtrusive aesthetic. Many believed the buildings would collapse after twenty years, yet they still remain an eyesore, and visible memory of the communist occupation. Situated on the farthest eastern reaches of the city, the buildings are strategically located next to a major economic source, the mining refinery.

Outside of these two walking tours, I had scheduled a day trip to Auschwitz. The largest German Nazi concentration camp and extermination center where over

1.1 million men, women and children lost their lives in Hitler's pursuit of the Final Solution to the Jewish question. A plan contrived by the National Socialist party in Germany to systematically exterminate the global population of Jews. I wanted to go there, to the site that now serves as a memorial and museum to remember, to pay homage to the lives lost and the symbolism of it all. I knew it wouldn't be an easy experience. It was very much like visiting the beaches of Normandy, where the allied infantry and armored divisions landed on the north coast of France, meeting fierce opposition by Germany's coastal battery. There was so much bloodshed and sacrifice; to say the experience was devastating only begins to describe the calamity. There are no words to adequately explain the wealth of emotions you face when you sign up for such an excursion. It was moving in a way that you feel your heart is being wrenched from your chest, tears swollen in your eyes at the immensity of innocent lives lost.

Returning from this solemn day outside the city, I found myself sitting on a concrete bench among the pigeons pecking at bread crumbs when I received a message from Kevin. I had put out a request for accommodation within the couch surfing community in this lively student town but had not heard any responses until now. I had already settled into my hostel, so there was no need for a place to stay, and frankly, Kevin wasn't offering room and board. What he was proposing was a night out on the town. After the heart-rending day reliving the history of Hitler's largest killing machine, I needed a break. I needed a time-out from thinking and more importantly feeling. I agreed to meet Kevin near St. Mary's Church in the old town center located on the main market square just in front of the Cloth Hall at nine.

I didn't know who I was exactly looking for or what to expect. Kevin is definitely not a Polish name, but it really didn't narrow down the search. Tall or short, young or old, okay I had a profile picture again, but it still didn't hinder me from starring down every person that passed by with an inquisitive eye, wondering, who it was I was waiting for.

Unlike a date, there was no pressure, no expectation that this was going anywhere in particular. We were two strangers meeting for a drink. What I would later find out was that one beer in a tucked-away bar off the main square was only a precursor to an entertaining night out on the town with Kevin, the guy with all the connections. Who knew Krakow was known to be one of the best party destinations in Europe? With a high concentration of bars and night clubs nestled down shady alleyways and buried in dark basements and cellars there was a labyrinth of places to lose yourself in only to resurface at daybreak with the rays of sun creeping over the rooftops blinding the bloodshot eyes.

Kevin, an Irishman, had been living in Poland for over a decade, and like most Irish liked a pint of beer. In fact, that is how he came to live in Krakow, an unlikely location to plant roots away from the emerald isle. Now he'd been here ten years enjoying a fruitful life in Poland.

One beer led to another. Funny the Irish, they are one of the friendliest nationalities I have met on my travels, always welcoming and typically they are genuinely concerned for others' well-being. My heart was finally on the mend, but still far from whole. I had grown tired of the same old story about why I was on this trip, where I was from and where I was going. Still wearing the scars of sadness on my face, I had to explain. My mind still toiled over mindless chatter of what if's and why's. It wasn't my intention to divulge all this information AGAIN to a complete stranger unaware of the baggage I was carrying. I knew my solemn mood could dampen the evening, but Kevin was a gentleman. (He will laugh when he reads that line.) He was exactly the person I needed to put life into perspective. He was straightforward and honest. He derived his advice from his own experiences. He too had gone through a recent breakup. See that is how the world should work, talking about our experiences, and ultimately helping others better traverse life. His inquisitiveness encouraged me to leave the past behind and start thinking about the future.

Kevin's story...he had moved to Poland on a whim. He was originally from a small town in the center of Ireland. He had lived on an island in the Mediterranean, and one day, he found himself in Krakow on business. After four hours in what was known to be an expat bar, he had been convinced to stay. It was no wonder that over the years he had created quite the name for himself, considering he walked out that day with an office, a network and a potential staff, everything he needed to transfer his activities to the mainland. Kevin is personable, the funny Irishman that everyone migrates to. As we entered the bars, he was acknowledged by bartenders, managers and staff. I felt like I was a celebrity being ushered to the front of the lines, greeting everyone Kevin introduced me to, but I wasn't dressed for such stardom. Wearing jeans and a t-shirt with a scarf flung around my neck, I felt inadequate and out-of-place as the girl on center stage.

It was about three in the morning when we walked up to the velvet rope that separated us from a very indiscriminate door. There were no neon signs or designation that this was anything more than a hole in a wall until the bouncer approached us in a sleek black suit and an earpiece. The owner of the club was nearby talking to a group of women when he recognized Kevin and sure enough, we were escorted in. Downstairs, a series of twists and turns. A cloakroom, toilets, one bar, a dance floor, more stairs. As we descended deeper, I wasn't quite sure how far underground we would go. We finally cozied up to a bar tucked off to the side of a hazy pass-through. The bar itself glowed a soft white in the dimly lit cellar space.

We were nearly the only customers down on this level. The owner made a point to accompany us to the bar and ordered a round of shots. Did I not mention that this was Poland? Up until now, I had not been introduced to this Polish hospitality, but it is a well-known fact that Poles like their vodka. With an average life expectancy of 90 years of age, there must be more to the proverb an apple a day will keep the doctor away.

Acknowledging that I was a foreigner and this could end very badly, the manager requested the bartender pour a fruity vodka infusion, which was much more palatable to my novice taste. But it was after a few of these rounds, the three of us with a line of twelve shot glasses on the rail, that I started to feel that it was time to throw the towel in for the night. Quickly I would come to regret this fun-filled evening in this fabled city if I didn't get some fresh air and a bite to eat.

Graciously I thanked my host for showing me the nightlife Krakow was known for. I would not have ventured out if it were not for Kevin's invitation. I liked to dine out on my own, but it was another thing to go to a club. One drink leads to another, and flying solo could have dangerous repercussions. Before parting ways, Kevin asked if I wanted to meet later in the week, not sure of his schedule, but if I fancied another rowdy night hopping in and out of lively watering holes, I should let him know. He would be around for the next week or two before he would head south. The boat, his floating address for much of the summer, was his "European adventure." Rather than going on some mission of self-discovery after his break up, he bought a boat, and not just some speed boat to take out to any one of the numerous lakes that dotted the Polish countryside, but a sailboat he used to navigate the high seas. Okay, that was definitely an outlet that would serve to free the mind from thoughts of the past. Considering he had very little knowledge of how to exactly sail a sailboat when he bought it, he was a quick learner hiring a certified instructor and taking it out for maneuvers in the dead of winter in the worst conditions. In a very short time, Kevin became quite a captain. If time did not allot for another drink in Krakow, I had an open invitation to call him on the HMS Everything Zen anchored in Croatia.

I made a mental note, tucking the thought of sailing in paradise in the back of my mind. I had never been sailing before. Living in Phoenix, I had owned a couple jet skis, but frankly, I was landlocked. I enjoyed the water, but living in the valley of the sun, the closest thing to spending time on the water was trekking the watercraft out to one of the nearby man-made lakes that canvased the vast desert land.

I wasn't quite sure of my itinerary for the rest of the summer. After Poland, I was heading to Ireland for three weeks exploring Kevin's motherland, and from there my plans had not yet been written.

I traveled to Ireland. I was sitting having a pint of Guinness at the St. James Brewery and Storehouse in Dublin overlooking the city from the fifth story Gravity Bar with floor to ceiling windows when my flight home to the United States departed from Paris. I had let my original return ticket lapse. I could only imagine my name being announced over the loudspeaker at the Charles de Gaulle Airport, and there was no one there to answer the call. My seat sat empty as I was lost in thought overlooking the sun-drenched buildings dotting the tiny streets crisscrossing Dublin that spread out below my feet. From this vantage point, I didn't know if I would ever return to the United States. Travel was starting to look good on me, and I had gotten used to its rhythms.

As I started to plan my next adventures, places to go, and people to see, Kevin's offer came to mind. Ireland, located in the northern reaches of Europe, was isolated. How would I manage to visit the many places of interest I had on mainland Europe and eventually find my way southeast to Croatia?

I sketched a plan. Money was not concerning me as I was still relying on my savings. I had budgeted for such extenuating circumstances and felt that my well-being was worth the investment. I would return to Belgium to revisit the friends I had made before. Kyle, the tour guide, had not yet drifted from my thoughts, and I wanted to see if what I left was a potential relationship or in fact the escalating feelings I felt would not be reciprocated. I needed more time in Belgium. I found a volunteer opportunity working with an English Youth camp in Flanders, where French-speaking students from Wallonia, in the south of Belgium were immersed in English. Playing American football, learning songs from the movie *Grease*, the camp offered fun activities married with classroom study. One of the teachers had already planned her summer holidays and invited me to tag along with her to Budapest. A girl's weekend away enjoying various renowned day spas that dotted this Hungarian capital. I would part from this friend and head back out on my own to Zurich, Switzerland then make my way south through Italy. As a trained chef and restauranteur, I wanted to indulge my senses on a culinary trek across the Italian countryside, from Como to Rome and places in between, discovering local specialties and regional favorites.

One thing unbeknownst to me, an American traveler, was that during the month of August, almost all Europeans take an extended holiday or vacation away from work. And by extended, I mean the entire month. This was especially true of the Italians. As I entered Modena, Italy, a city known for its decadent aged balsamic vinegar and sports car manufacturing like Ferrari, the streets were empty. I stepped off the train at the main station into a ghost town expecting tumbleweeds to pass by in the scorching heat. Shutters locked tight and blinds pulled, "chiusa," closed signs hung in café windows. I quickly started to reformulate my plans. Before leaving the United States on this venture, Croatia hadn't crossed my mind, but now why not?

Passenger ferries departed daily from the industrial port town Ancona, along the Italian coast, to the vibrant tourist destination Split, situated straight line across the Adriatic Sea along the colorful Croatian seaboard defined by numerous islands and natural wonders. In five hours, I could be sailing the pristine waters with Kevin enjoying fresh sea breezes and cold beers under a sheer blanket of warm sunshine.

I reached Ancona late in the afternoon. The heat radiating from the concrete, every step felt like I was walking on a bed of sweltering coals. The train had been packed full of beach goers and backpackers looking for recourse from the summer heat along the sea, dispensing its contents one beach bar after another. Ancona, the final stop, was a dust blown concrete jungle. As an industrial harbor, the town was very different from the picturesque beaches we had passed on the way. Envy aside, I would only be staying one night in what felt like an abandoned one-horse town in a Hollywood Western. No beach could compare; I was on my way to a floating paradise washed in golden light.

I had called my father from an internet café near the railway station. I hadn't spoken to him since he flew back to the United States from Paris. Three months had nearly passed since, and it dawned on me that I had not reached out to anyone for some time. When I said I was incognito, I meant it. Outside of the pictures I posted along my travels, the outside world had no clue to my whereabouts. I liked it that way, though I did have this eerie feeling that I could cease to exist and no one would inquire to my whereabouts for months. With that thought in mind, I concluded it may be time to check-in.

I was tucked in a muggy cubicle with a phone receiver close to my ear. I entertained my father on the other end of the line with the adventures I had been on and the ones I was yet to take. I was embarking on an experience that for some would seem crazy, dangerous or just plain stupid.

To most "normal" people boarding a stranger's sailboat for a week sounds absurd. Okay, maybe I too questioned my state of sanity, but I still went for it. I trusted my intuition, at least in part. I knew it was a bit of a gamble. An opportunity like this was rare, and I wasn't about to let it pass me by without at least giving it a chance.

When I hung up the receiver, I felt a sense of relief. My father, though he probably couldn't point Croatia out on the map, did know the approximate vicinity I would be in if anything would go awry. Settling into bed that night I couldn't stop tossing and turning, wrestling with the raucous echoing from the street below, and the summer heat permeating like a furnace from every hard stone surface in sight. My skin was balmy, lying on top of a sheet as I closed my eyes, coaxing my thoughts into dreams as I fell into a deep slumber.

With the sun creeping through the open window, I slowly began to stretch my arms. Most of my belongings were already packed as the ferry would depart not long after daybreak. Quickly I showered and dropped the keys at the reception before walking out into the sunlight.

After a 25-minute walk to the ticket office, I boarded a bus to shuttle the crowd from the shipyard offices to the departures terminal. This was all new to me. In all my travels, I hadn't even boarded a cruise ship before. Having already scouted out the harbor and ferry marina, a vast maze of docks and towering elevators to load and unload ships, I would have been lost in the morning bustle. At this point, Croatia had not yet entered the European Union and was not a member of the Schengen community. What this meant for me and my fellow passengers was standing in yet another queue to get our passports stamped. A daunting process of hurry up and wait, where you followed the line of other travelers, mostly Italians, rolling their suitcases around the stern of the ship to the staircase leading up into the hull.

As I took the first step onto the high-speed ferry, my anticipation greatened. By noon I would be disembarking in Croatia joining Kevin in the marina where he would be readying the boat with supplies.

My first impressions of Croatia were that of a bustling port with an adjacent bus terminal, little fast food shops and street vendors. It felt like I was struggling through throngs of mayhem, everyone trying to edge their way to somewhere else making little to no headway. It was much like Brussels Midi Market where all likes of people come to shop, elbowing to the front of lines to get their weekly assortment of fresh produce without reverence for their fellow shoppers. Passersby thrust their loot from left to right all while pushing their trollies and children's strollers over foot and paw. It is grungy, crowded and eclectic. A good mood could easily be spoiled by impatience, but hey, everyone should experience this sort of ordered chaos at least once in their lives.

I had directions to follow the boardwalk around, a twenty-minute walk to the marina where I would find Kevin packed and ready to go. As I walked, I was taking in my new surroundings. Along the "riva," the boardwalk, there was a stage being constructed for a weekend festival. Kids played, and a lively group of older locals gathered around two park benches singing traditional songs merrily passing the day. I was already falling in love.

As I made my way out of the old town, I found the marina which was directly across the harbor from where I had arrived. Sure enough, there was Kev.

This wasn't a date, nor did I have any intention for it to be one. Funny, always there with a story to tell, Kevin is one of a kind, with a genuine heart and a man who loves a party. What elevates him in my eyes is he is more like my older, much wiser brother rather than boyfriend. Even though it was just the two of us out at sea, it was as if two old friends from years gone by met in passing on a street corner somewhere and couldn't stop chatting away about their life's experiences depicting the good, bad and the humiliating with wildly vivid detail.

What I had feared most was not so much the fact that I had only met Kevin once, but was actually the contrary. We had hit it off months ago in Krakow, but that was just for drinks. What made me fret was that we were on a boat, and there was no escape. We either had to get along and enjoy one another's company or dwell in sweat and misery for an entire week at sea.

Kevin fortunately lived up to his Irish roots. After traveling across his motherland for three weeks, I had grown fond of Irish hospitality. Kevin was just as down to earth and sincere as he had been in Krakow, and it made me feel relaxed. I could open up to him about my concerns about my present situation without fear of judgement. Though last fringes of the breakup still lingered in my mind, it wasn't that which was disconcerting. Rather, what loomed over my head was what I was supposed to do with my life next.

Croatia had not been on my agenda, nor had I intended to meet anyone with such a genuine interest in my well-being. This was what I had been waiting for the entire summer, the unexpected that would eventually inspire a change in my life that would take my mere existence to an entirely new level.

Over the past few months, I felt like a recorder stuck on repeat. Playing over and over the same depressing country song to one innocent bystander after another. My lyrics had changed slightly becoming more detailed as I relived the past, but the subject matter stayed the same. I would have to applaud Kevin that he had the patience to put up with me the first couple of days where I consistently drew upon our conversation from before, dwelling on the what-if's and could-have-been's.

Along the way Kevin miraculously broke me from my funk, and I wasn't dealing with mild bouts of depression anymore. One morning we were docked near Hvar, one of Croatia's many popular island destinations known for lavish parties and fashionable clubs. It was the place to be for those wanting a good time. The marina we managed to get a spot in was full of boats. Flags of various colors flew high in the sky from Germany, Australia, Italy, from all over really. I could hear so many languages being spoken on neighboring boats, not knowing what exactly I was hearing. Bright and early people would wake for breakfast, running to the showers and picking up supplies from the little whitewashed hut stocked with necessities to get those passing through onto their next destination.

After a few days of being out to sea, I had got accustomed to Kevin's routine, more of a ritual in fact. As the captain, we moved at his pace, and he was definitely more a night owl than an early riser. After a refreshing morning swim in the cool, tranquil water surrounding the little island that was adjacent to Hvar, I grabbed a quick shower and a cup of coffee.

The sun was warm overhead as I sat down to a good book waiting for my jolly captain to awake from his slumber. I could get used to this life, working remotely under the clear blue sky with gentle sea breezes caressing my cheek, eating the local catch of the day from any one of the family-run restaurants and cafes that dotted the waterfront. Life was good; I was without worry, adrift, a vagabond, but I knew this fairytale would have to come to an end soon. I would eventually have to grudgingly return to the real world whether I liked it or not.

Before I laid eyes on the weary master of the ship, I heard him rustling below deck. Soon enough, we would set sail for the afternoon en route to our next destination. As Kevin climbed the steps up to the sun-drenched deck where I sat perched on a beach towel and a pile of ropes connected to the sail, he asked if I wanted to go for a light breakfast gesturing at the nearby fisherman's hole.

Over the last few days, we had talked about my future. Having worked hard over the past decade or so in the hospitality industry, I had been relying on my earnings to pay for this trip. As the days and weeks drew near, I knew this blasé lifestyle would fade into a memory, and I was starting to get nervous. I had stowed away this financial cushion as my rainy-day fund. As Kevin put it into perspective, there would be no better time to chart out a new course and invest in myself than the present, and that is exactly what I had been saving for. This trip constituted an investment, a change of course that came at a cost.

Toying with a plethora of thoughts, Kevin could sense something was on my mind and was bound to get to the bottom of it. He had an inherent way of drawing out information I wanted to keep buried. Understand this, I didn't want to return to the United States. Frankly, it made my belly turn thinking about it. I felt safe and at home in Europe. Over the previous four months, I had made a wealth of friends across a variety of countries, in particular, Belgium.

I know what you are thinking, it was for a guy, right? I was still madly in love with Kyle. Wrong. After Joshua, I had made a pact, I would never lose myself in a relationship again. I would not be moving an entire continent to be with a man. It was more than that. It was the friends that I had made along the way who inspired me to create a change in my life. They welcomed me into their lives like I was a member of their families and made me feel important. I felt supported in a way I had never experienced before.

Wanting to stay, I couldn't figure out the logistics. I had been online looking for jobs thinking that if I could solidify employment, it would be easier to apply for residency. Immigration to Europe was not as simple as moving coast to coast or from state to state for that matter. Immigration policies since 9/11 were stringent, and the paperwork was daunting.

Kevin was onboard with my thought process. He had heard me talk fondly about Belgium and my experiences there, but he was also thinking realistically. Belgium was not an English-speaking country. It would be hard as an American whose language skills were solely English to find a job. French and/or Dutch would almost always be required in the workplace, and I was terribly lacking in those departments.

What about Australia? Out of nowhere, Kevin threw a wild card on the table, an English-speaking country that wasn't the United States. He had a good friend move there some years back thinking she would only stay a year and then return to Poland, but she never did. She fell in love with Australia, like being seduced by the man of her dreams. Earning a comfortable living, making friends and enjoying life near the beach, she had all that she desired.

Australia had always topped my list of places I wanted to visit someday, but now it became one of two places that I would actually consider relocating to. Even though I had never been there myself, I had met many Australians on my travels. What was concerning wasn't so much making friends but finding a place I felt like I was home in. Melbourne was far different than Sydney on many levels from sports and entertainment to cost of living and weather. Without a personal frame of reference, I wouldn't be able to judge from pictures alone on the internet or hear-say to make that type of decision without first-hand experience on the ground.

Playing with these thoughts was invigorating. I had been lost for so long, complacent in both my personal and professional life that the map of my future was starting to unfold in front of me. Wondering and looking for purpose was never something I was good at, but now I could feel that there was magic in the air. I was heading in the right direction with my thoughts and aspirations, and the way I knew this was that I had this overwhelming sense of peace within my heart. Of course, there was a hint of fear; either decision would be a significant leap of faith. Moving to Belgium or Australia were two countries far away from the place I had once called home. I would be out on my own facing uncertainty at every angle. If I failed, it wouldn't be so easy to pack it all up and lick my wounds.

Kevin acknowledged this. He weighed out my options and the level of risk each presented, and Belgium was in the lead. Though Australia was a good choice, in theory, it was much farther away and quite remote. The immigration process would be easier, yes, but there wasn't any *one* person or group of people whom I could rely on to help me in my transition. I had friends, of course, but I had met them years ago on my travels and really didn't feel confident that they would extend a caring hand in the same way I was assured of Belgium.

Kevin, not having been to Belgium, had no insight on the subject, but what he could confess was that after hearing me talk through my issues over the past week, he was convinced that my soul would not find solace if I did not run the risk.

WISDOM 1 EVALUATE THE OPTIONS

It may not have been wise to put myself in possible danger, jumping on a sailboat with Kevin, but I have never once regretted the decision. He has turned out to be one of my best friends. He was and still is that motivating force that inspires me to evaluate my options and take chances.

If it were not for Kevin, I may never have entertained the idea that I could make such a drastic change in my life. That I would adamantly reject every caution flag that would have confined me to the life I once knew, and embark on an even greater adventure than the one I was on, with no beacon to guide my way.

Toying with an idea, an aspiration or a dream? What is stopping you from seeing it to fruition? Let me guess, could it be fear, ambition, lack of funding, a relationship, parents, siblings or something else that you imagine is holding you back?

Be brave, trust yourself, thwart off caution and courageously break away from the status quo, because you are not fully living until you do.

Weigh your options. I do this all the time. Know your comfort level and rise above it. Failure is not the end of the world but rather a chance to learn and grow. When you put things into perspective, you have a clearer picture of every scenario and can wager the options you have. It is my hope that you choose the option that offers the highest growth potential. If you look at personal development as a positive outcome from your endeavor, whatever it may be, you will not digress into a state of fear.

Change, although scary, is healthy. Here is a bit of advice. Don't overestimate what can go wrong. When we focus on the negative, we magnify it in our imaginations and often manifest it in our lives. The probability of something going wrong is minimal, think of it in that sense.

If your imagination is anything like mine, then it is rather uninhibited and capable of mustering the most catastrophic consequences if we allow it to roam freely, but the truth is, we always have more control of the outcome than we inherently think.

Most of us underestimate our own ability to persevere and see our initiatives through. As humans, we constantly feed into our vulnerabilities, drowning in self-doubt, though if we took a clear look at our lives and past experiences, we would see all the challenges we have overcome as a testament to our strength and tenacity in times of change and difficulty. Don't sell yourself short. The consequences of inaction are that you will never live up to your full potential, that life will only ever be good enough, but never great, never outstanding. Where is the fun in being "sensible" all the time? Calculate the risk, and if you can manage the odds, go for your dreams.

CHAPTER 8

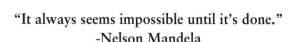

WHERE'S HOME?

"It always seems impossible until it's done."
-Nelson Mandela

Cooler temperatures meant the season was changing; October had arrived. I had been back in the United States for over a month and a half. I had interviewed with so many restaurants, resorts and bars that I started to lose count. Day after day, I sat in front of my computer looking through want ads. I had moved from my friend's townhome into a small two-bedroom house located in one of Phoenix's suburbs I rented with a young mother looking for a roommate. I was starting a new life. One restaurant group even had me board a plane for an interview in Santa Monica. A 5-hour on-the-job interview, what we in the industry refer to as a "stage" or "stagiaire" was a trial run, hands-on working interview to demonstrate your abilities and qualifications in a fully operational restaurant. Wanting to stay in Los Angeles for a few more hours was just not plausible. The director of the HR department dropped me off at the departures terminal of LAX, and I was back in Phoenix by nightfall.

My best efforts to integrate back into society after being gone for almost a half a year were waning. I was searching for my calling, what it was that I was supposed to do with my life, now that I fully embraced a new chapter with a clear mind and open heart. I had changed significantly over the five months I had spent traveling on my own, and I no longer fit inside the circles I once kept. Friends felt distant. I was unable to relate on many levels because my experiences acted like a wedge. When I spoke of my travels I was not trying to flaunt or rub it in that I was able to see the world, and they were not, but it often felt like I further dissociated myself the more I recounted my expedition abroad. I felt like I had to limit these conversations. In order to fit in, I couldn't stand out. My travels made me unique, but in my circle of friends, or maybe they were more acquaintances, I unconsciously set myself apart and felt guilty. I reprimanded myself for pursuing my aspirations.

I wanted to fit in, and I tried. I thought to myself, just maybe if I were to find the right job, with the right company that I would also find peace, but the task was daunting. One opportunity after another, nothing seemed to be the right fit. It was like going into a dress shop and trying on the entire inventory only to leave empty-handed.

At some point, I just stopped trying. There was no point looking at want ads, scheduling interviews, or signing a new lease to an apartment I didn't want. The beauty of the rental agreement I signed on the house was that it was flexible, not tying me down for any determined period of time. I spoke to my roommate and what it all came down to was I didn't feel at home in Phoenix, plain and simple, but would jumping state borders really make a difference? I felt my calling was lost somewhere out there.

For the most part, I returned to the life I had once known. It was the same life I was trying to get away from when I had departed for Europe, the same faces, places and routines that had caused me to seek change in the first place.

Throughout all my travels abroad out on my own, I never felt as isolated as I did when I came home.

After I left Croatia, I returned to Italy, continuing my descent south to Florence, Sienna and finally Rome. You'll remember from the beginning of this tale, I was lost in Sienna with Laura the day before the Palio horse race. It was the end of August, around the time of my birthday that I decided to catch one more flight from Rome to Brussels. I had no intrinsic connection to Rome. A city steeped in magnificent works of art, religion and ancient ruins was immensely fascinating, but I knew no one and would be alone if I decided to stay. Rather than celebrate the 27th anniversary of my birth with strangers, I opted to go "home," but home may not be what you are thinking. I wasn't going back to the United States but rather Belgium, back to those friends who made me feel so welcome and accepted.

I flew back into Brussels Charleroi after taking the 6 am flight out of Rome Fiumicino. Waiting there in the arrivals gate was my friend Lize who would take me back to the barracks, the apartment buildings used by the US military to house the soldiers stationed in the city either working for NATO or the US Army Garrison. Crashing a friend's couch, I had five days left in Europe before I would catch a flight back through New York to visit family before making my way onto Phoenix.

We had a spectacular weekend planned, both Lize and I had birthdays to celebrate. She had made arrangements to celebrate on Friday in Brussels, and we would continue the festivities on into Saturday by carpooling up to Bruges, the city where I had started my summer adventures abroad after leaving my disgruntled father at the airport in Paris.

Sobering up from Friday night's shenanigans, a group of guys and I thought it was a good idea to combat the impending hangover with shots of Jack Danial's at 10 am and scrambled eggs, setting the stage for the rest of the day. I had friends come in from London and make their way to Bruges by train. We all gathered in the hotel before heading out on a tour of the Halve Man Brewery where we proceeded to continue our exploits, becoming very boisterous, beer after mouthwatering beer.

Dinner reservations were arranged at a popular rib joint frequented by locals and tourists alike. After licking our fingers, consuming our fill of all-you-can-eat BBQ we made our way, a big group of twenty-some's, along cobblestone streets through the Grote Markt dominated by the 12th century belfry and Provincial Court down the road to the St. Christopher Backpacker's Bar where my military friends' sole mission that night was to get me exceptionally drunk. They would not stop feeding me shots of tequila until I raised the white flag, or more truthfully fell off the curb in a drunken stumble, and they decided it was time to call it a night and carried me back to our hotel. I had lost the battle and passed out unconscious until morning when I found myself alone under crisp white sheets in my own room. Others had a rough night as well. We looked dreadful, a sorry lot of unkept vagrant as we made our way downstairs to breakfast, where the smell of eggs made me nauseous.

There was about a dozen of us in total. Splitting up among three cars, the soberest individuals among us drove home where we would nurse our throbbing heads back to health with pizza delivery, curled up on the couch watching reruns of *Shameless* from one my friends' DVD collections.

My flight was scheduled; I knew the inevitable loomed over my head. I would have to say my goodbyes and return to the States. Literally, my days were numbered. I had stayed 90 days in the Schengen and almost a month and a half outside in the United Kingdom, Ireland and Croatia. Legally I would have to go and let another 90 days pass before I could even entertain returning.

Flying over the Rockies into Phoenix Sky Harbor Airport, I heard the voice over the intercom inform the flight crew to prepare for landing. I had thought nothing of the five-hour flight from New York's JFK until we were only twenty minutes away from touching the wheels down on the asphalt runway when a jolt of emotion blindsided me. Never having dealt with anxiety, I found myself short of breath with a belly full of knots wrapping my arms around my stomach. All of a sudden, I felt this intense notion that I wanted to run away, to turn in the opposite direction and sprint, but where to? I couldn't just rush off into thin air. Fear. Fear of the unknown was the root to my unsettled nerves. Months of nomadic travel changed me in such a way that I no longer knew if I would fit in the bubble I once called my life.

Kevin kept up with my progress checking in every other day to see how I was doing and if I had given any more thought about returning to Europe more permanently. It felt like I had this guardian angel with a mischievous side hovering over my shoulder, guiding my every move. Prodding me to relinquish ties and run full force into a future not yet revealed to me.

In mid-October, as the trees were changing color, I returned to Iowa for my brother's going away party. It would be his second tour of duty in the Middle East, one he had made himself viable for. See, the military suited my brother, and my brother suited the military. Smart, level-headed, and efficient under extreme pressure, Dustin had completed advanced training that made him a desirable candidate for this twelve-month mission into the mountainous terrain of Afghanistan.

My father organized a farewell party at home, entertaining a host of family and friends I wouldn't miss. I was always immensely proud of my brother for the decisions he made in his life. Even as a teenager, I looked up to him, always getting good grades and excelling at whatever he put his mind to. He was calm, cool and someone I could always rely on. One day in my sophomore year in high school, I got called to the principal's office. I was told that my brother was hanging a garage door at the student-built house on the outer edge of town. A routine procedure went awry when the metal wire that connected the wheels of the door to the track snapped wrapping itself around my brother's pinky. In the matter of mere seconds, his finger popped off under the force of the metal. They said he was found standing holding his bloodied hand in the air. I was in shock, a flush of blood went swirling to my head as I thought about the accident, but I was assured by the school administrator all was well.

The teacher had reacted quickly ushering Dustin to the school's work truck fitted with toolboxes, yelling at a nearby student to pick up the last digit of my brother's finger before rushing off to the hospital. All the while, Dustin was conscious. He lost his finger; the doctors were unable to unite the severed skin with the stump that remained. Did this stop him? Not at all. Determined to complete the task, he returned to the building site to render his service and continue construction of the home. I was proud of his accomplishments. When my relationship with our father wavered, he stepped in as my guardian and protector. I don't remember the facts clearly, a moment from my past I have washed from my memory.

The next week I interviewed with a chef-owned restaurant group that had open call interviews in Scottsdale. Walking into a meeting room filled with other candidates, I was neck to neck with my competition vying for an upper-level management position. With my resume tucked in the black leather folder on my lap, I sat there ready and waiting.

I played the same old game answering the questions about operations and my experiences in the food and beverage industry as though the answers were written on the back of my hand. I could go through the process eyes closed, walking straight forward to the finish line. The hospitality industry was so familiar to me that I had the right answer to every problem or query presented.

When I entered the elevator to leave, I knew it was over. Something had clicked inside. The fact that I had every answer mapped out like a playbook was the defining moment. Within this industry, I could be successful, but I no longer felt like I was offered room to grow. I, of course, could take a higher salary or a new title, but I no longer felt the challenge to move up the corporate ladder.

If there was one turning point, it was this; I decided to move to Brussels.

It would be a shocking blow to my father. Not only would he be sending his son off to the conflicts in the Middle East, but he would also have to wish his daughter farewell on her new exciting venture. I am not sure what he feared more, the prospect of his son not returning from the battlefield or that his little girl may find her place abroad and never return to the life he had once wished for her.

Even though we did not have the traditional father-daughter relationship, it did mean something to me that he wished me well. I knew my family wasn't terribly surprised at my decision, whether they believed I would be successful in my pursuits or not. I had lived and worked in Europe and, now with this last brief stint abroad, a short-lived adventure over a five-month period they thought it might be a phase I was going through, a quarter-life crisis that would soon pass. Wishing me the best, I think they were holding their breath that things wouldn't work out as I planned. At least that was the perception I was getting from the crowd of family and friends that made it to my brother's farewell party that turned into "our" send-off.

Excitement was mounting. I had bought my tickets days after returning to Phoenix from Iowa. With my flight confirmation sitting in my inbox, there was a whole list of things to do before my scheduled departure. I was moving to Europe! I wasn't sure if I would be gone for months or for years. If I would fail or succeed. I had to make arrangements in hopes that it would be the latter, that my biggest risk would ultimately lead to my biggest accomplishment, a life-changing conquest.

Hosting garage sales and putting my possessions in the want ads was only the start of a very enlightening process of putting my life in order. I no longer needed the material possessions I had once deemed the utter definition of my life's worth. Over the past months, I came to realize I could live with far less and be just as comfortable if not more. My life no longer valued things but treasured relationships that fostered growth and understanding.

This period was a time of immense change and reflection. Tidying up loose ends and closing doors, the anticipation was mounting to begin the next chapter of my life. That's when I met him.

It was a surprise actually that I was even attracted to this man. I was at an impromptu pool party in November. Yes, I know it sounds odd. An old roommate, a DJ friend of mine, Brent had invited me after work to a house he was taking care of while the owners were away. They had given him the keys and told him to have a good time, and so he did literally, throwing small casual gatherings nearly every night of the week while the owners were away. I wasn't expecting to meet anyone, as the story goes, it was a small gathering of people from work, most of whom I knew, but one person, in particular, drew my attention. Before I had left on my five-month adventure across Europe, I had met him briefly in passing. It turned out we actually worked for the same restaurant group, only in different locations making it quite impossible for our paths to cross.

I had come into my own over the summer, and with this upcoming move to look forward to, I felt empowered. Describing it is hard, but I was radiating my more feminine side. I was sensual and flirtatious. Could I go so far as to say that my ego got the better of me? The drinks flowed, and before dawn broke over the horizon, I was swimming nude, unstrapping my bra and flinging my black lace thong onto a sun chair before making a splash into the deep end. This action caused a positive reaction inspiring others to do the same, freeing themselves of their conservative attire and openly baring all.

I wasn't hiding the fact that I was leaving the United States in a little over a month. With no intentions or expectations, I think that was what made it so much fun.

Stephen, five years my junior, was not exactly the man I would typically fall head over heels for. He was really not my type at all. With an average height, athletic build, sandy blonde hair, blue eyes and a scruffy chin, he was the exact opposite to those men I had fancied before. I always fell for the tall, dark, handsome man that was more in love with himself than his prey. I guess in some regard I was finally breaking up the routine and forming some new habits, at least in the area of men.

One of my favorite things about this relationship was that everything was new. I saw life through a whole new set of eyes. There were no expectations, no titles and no plans for the future. We were living in the passion. I had never lived like this before, without limits. I felt committed and free at the same time. An affair that had an expiration date agreed upon from the start. Before I was always concerned with the unknown and the fact that I was dependent on the love and acceptance of another.

We had made a pact one night after we both got off work, having met for a couple of beers in a local microbrewery downtown. I had a grand idea. I wanted to do something I had never done before.

Waking just before dawn on Christmas Day, the freeway was wide open as families gathered around the Christmas tree singing carols; we were headed north to Flagstaff, Arizona. A crisp chill was in the air as the sun crept over the horizon and golden rays of light glistened across the freeway. When we neared our destination, we were welcomed by falling snowflakes and traces of snow and pine along the side of the road. We were heading in the direction of the San Francisco Peaks, a ridge of four hills that characterize the farthest reaches of the Rocky Mountains in Arizona located just west of the bustling university town.

I had never been snowboarding before, skiing, yes, but it had been a horrible experience, a catastrophe actually. I had been in Winter Park-Fraser, Colorado, many years ago, when I tried the sport. Without any lessons or guidance, I took the lift up the slope. Descending at an unfathomably slow pace, I would purposefully fall over every few minutes to deter from gaining too much speed. I was scared and embarrassed so much that it detracted the good from the experience. I was with a big group of college friends who were far more trained than me. Needless to say, the next day, my inhibitions caused me to turn in my skis for a snowmobile and once again, all was right in the world.

Rather than revisiting memory lane I wanted to learn, actually get lessons on how to properly snowboard safely and have some fun. Strapping on my rented board, maneuvering with one-foot sliding across the compacted snow to the lifts, I climbed up on the seat with Stephen at my side. Well, I didn't exactly get professional training. I trusted my education on this matter to Stephen. He was patient and thorough, giving me tricks and tips on how to get down the mountain without falling, keeping my head and eyes up and following the direction of my gaze at all times.

I had never had so much fun playing in the snow. I fell, that was inevitable, but I didn't have a problem getting back on my feet. Gaining speed, I thought I had the hang of it, well at least until midafternoon when I graduated from the amateur's green slope. Surprisingly I thought I had the knack for snowboarding. Stephen showered me in compliments as we moved in another direction, to bigger, better, steeper runs. That was when it happened.

Losing my footing on the compacted snow, my board flew out from under me as I was trying to ease my way down a narrow catwalk. I was stunned, not sure what hit me when my tailbone collided with the ice undertow. A piercing pain shot up my spine. I was on my back looking up at the pine trees overhead. I couldn't move. Faintly I could hear, "Are you okay up there?" Stephen was calling out from a distance, his voice muffled by other snowboarders cutting down the mountain. The curve edged up to a steep cliff I was lucky not to have fallen over. If there was a bright side, this was it. Lying there motionless trying to regain my composure, it felt as if the wind had been knocked from my lungs while getting kicked as hard as possible at the base of my spine.

All I could think was breathe, just breathe, inhale, exhale, it will be okay, just breathe. I lifted my chest just enough to see over the ridge down at the man who stared back up at me with considerable worry and concern. "Just give me five." I just need five minutes, and I would force myself to get up on my feet and resume my downhill descent.

Leaving not so fond of a memory, the pain and agony lasted nearly a week. With the help of a couple of spiked hot cocoas, I am proud to say I did board the rest of that Christmas day. I was moving a bit more cautiously of course but moving none-the-less.

When we hung up our mittens for the day, and we returned our equipment to the local shop, we set out to find a hotel and restaurant to continue our informal holiday celebrations.

Sinking into a hot bubble bath, Stephen was there to massage my aches and pains, kissing my shoulders and sliding his body in next to mine. I had never felt so comfortable with a man as I sunk into his arms that pulled me close. I never tired of his embrace, as he satisfied my every want and desire.

As the days approached my impending departure date, I started to look at things differently. My eyes fell upon longtime friends that I might not see for a while. I don't believe in goodbyes, but I had this overarching feeling that time would pass before we would meet again.

After living in Phoenix for nearly eight years, I had once thought I had seen and experienced it all. Taking a closer look, I had hardly skimmed the surface, and there was a small part of me that would be sad to go.

This so-called "leap of faith," as I referenced it, would not be easy. Leaving all the familiarity of a place I once considered home and the security of having a job and place to lay my head, I was one of the lucky ones to have friends on the receiving end to welcome me into their lives and offer a place for me to stay while I figured things out. I wasn't blindly marching off into my future but rather taking a calculated risk on myself.

Who sets out to move abroad without a clear plan anyway? I asked myself this so many times like an actress trying to perfect her lines. It sounded courageous and incomprehensible at the same time. I guess that was what so many of my friends believed. When my going-away party arrived, many people I had invited were unable to attend. Of course, I was disheartened, these individuals had meant something to me. Maybe they thought my dreams were just that, dreams and my imaginative balloon would soon be popped, and I would fall back to reality. But what they didn't know was that I was bound, no determined, to prove them wrong. I had made my decision, and now it was time to see if it would come to fruition.

Stephen was there in the end. Of course he was. By this time, we had fallen for one another. It wasn't planned. Getting our emotions involved wouldn't lead us to any good. Both of us would end up losing a battle we hadn't intended to fight. It would make boarding the plane that much harder, knowing I couldn't stay even for his love. We never said anything about our feelings, but we knew they were there, a yearning to be together and everyone could see it.

Stephen helped pack the final household belongings I still had into a storage unit. I wasn't sure that I would find my place abroad and wanted to leave behind a cushion to fall back on if things did not turn out as planned. I still had my car, a five-year-old black Volkswagen Jetta I needed to get rid of, eliminating both insurance and storage cost, adding to my savings. As the last grain of sand fell from the hourglass, time had run out. Stephen would sell it after I left. Friends thought I had to be crazy, allowing a man I had only dated for a month and half to have the title and license to my car, but I trusted him with the responsibility. I received an email a little over two months later that I would be happy about the person he sold the car to. It was a father and son. The father wanted his son to learn how to drive a manual. A smile dawned on my face. The decision was very fitting as I had once confided to Stephen that the first car I bought with my own money I couldn't even drive off the lot. It too was a manual, and who else was to teach me but my own father. I guess it was a rite of passage I was happy to know someone else would experience.

For a couple of months, Stephen and I exchanged a few emails and once or twice spoke on the phone, but that was it. We both knew it would eventually come to an end. As much as I thought he had fallen madly in love, I think

I was deeper. I went so far as to express my feelings in a letter I mailed to his home only to find out he was dating someone new, and rightfully so. How naïve was I to think that things could somehow work between us? He wasn't going to put his life on hold to come to Europe, and I wasn't about to throw away my dreams on a chance relationship. There it was. As much as I wanted it all, I had to let go.

WISDOM 1 LIVING WITH DISCOMFORT

What happens next? You made a bet and gambled on chance. You jumped into the great void, living life in no-man's land, or limbo, as I have come to term it. A place that is neither here, nor there. You have set sail like so many wise men and women have before charting out new waters away from the coast, but yet your destination is not quite in sight. You feel like you're drowning at times, struggling to persevere and in other moments everything will coast along at a steady rate, and you will wonder why you hadn't released the chains that confined you earlier.

Embracing change and accepting discomfort when you feel like you're being drug under a swell is not for the weary. Trepidation is normal when you are waiting for your intentions to come to fruition. If you allow it, you can lose sight of these goals and deviate off course, even back to the safe harbor you once came. I could have easily taken a new job in the valley but to what avail, I would have been living inside the parameters of comfort, bored with life. Jumping into the deep was the only recourse.

One thing I want to make very clear is that you have to get comfortable with the discomfort or it has the capacity to swallow you whole. Whether it is quitting your job and investing in your own business or moving across the country, there will always be a period of adjustment or unease between point A and point B. Always remember that. You cannot leave the steady and predictable rhythms of life you once knew and expect everything to stay the same. You have to create a new flow without having instructions to guide you.

Don't be distraught. Imagine you are out at sea, the waves may be great, but there is a warm sun overhead drenching you in golden light. There will always be light in the midst of adversity and distress, just hang on and don't lose sight of its grace.

Blessed by a wealth of individuals who I met on my travels across Europe, I was kept on course. Through their encouragement and example, I was able to plant roots in a more fertile soil that supported my growth and well-being.

A great practice when times get tough, and you are not quite sure if you want to turn back to the comfort and the stability of the past, remind yourself why you took the first step out on the hire wire, daring to create the life you have always dreamed. Most likely, you won't really like what you see in the rearview mirror.

Don't let the pressure of the big picture overwhelm you and take life in stride. Look for blessings or "the light" in the every day as you chart your new course, and let this serve as a reminder that you are heading in the right direction. Whether those blessings are new acquaintances, experiences or serendipitous happenings, let them guide you forward, leaving the past where it is meant to stay.

CHAPTER 9

WHY BELGIUM?

"There can be no great accomplishment without risk."
-Neil Armstrong

Five months had passed to no avail. From a place of spiritual being, of complete silence, I became aware of a calling, a voice, telling me to go for it, to seek my truth exactly where I thought I would find it. I have no better way to describe it, God didn't speak to me directly telling me to go out and be a shepherd, but I knew I had to make a decision that would ultimately change my future. What lay beyond this choice would dare to challenge my persistence and patience, but in the end, would reap reward. Like a buried treasure, some higher power had given me means to become aware that this desire would only be satisfied if I were to let go of the past that was binding and jump into the abyss, or at least that was how I felt. I took a leap into the unknown with only faith in the Lord and the universe to guide me.

There is no better way to explain the next few months. After arriving in the worst winter conditions, snow and sleet caked the streets, the cobblestones were torturous, making every step an effort. I wondered what I had bought into. What kind of dream was this? I had left the sun-kissed desert where there were only ever two seasons, hot and very hot for this? I had to bundle up wrapping my scarf around my neck and pulling my hood down toward my eyes. Knee-high boots and leather gloves completed the ensemble. Any part of the body left visible to the subzero conditions ran a risk of getting frostbite.

Short periods of depression and culture shock plagued my days. I slept late battling what I referred to as jet lag, but this time warp could only last so long. A month of jet lag was merely an excuse disguising a bigger issue. I was deathly scared, so much that it limited my productivity. I had no job, no permanent residence and was at the whim of the authorities as to whether I would be granted the right to stay in Belgium. Not to mention, thoughts of Stephen tormented my conscience. Would my gamble be worth the cost? A relationship that had fallen victim to the game I played.

I didn't have the answers. I was the type to always have a plan. As much as I wanted to be that happy-go-lucky type of girl, I worried. I had always landed the serious role in life. I was able to take advantage of moments of spontaneity, usually when alcohol was involved, but for the most part, I was predictable. This was about to change. I was an outsider trying to get in, and what was troubling was I had to find the right key to unlock the door.

The days were short, and the dark grey skies were not the ideal welcome I had anticipated. What was I expecting? This wasn't the French Riviera. Northern Europe wasn't going to offer the sandy, golden beaches and characteristic Mediterranean climate that could be found in say Spain or Italy. Belgium was never a country adored for its climate, far from it actually. The year I arrived, it was reported to have been the worst winter in recent history. The combination of below-average temperatures, rain, sleet and snow couldn't get worse. The longevity of such extreme conditions even ruffled the seasoned locals.

Fortunately, as the first month began to pass, I started to get my senses about me. I was overwhelmed by the kindness shown by the friends I had made on my travels. This social network made the world of a difference; without them, I don't think any of this would have ever been possible. Where I am today is a product of their generosity and compassion.

Americans, Belgians, Dutch, Germans, Norwegians, Italians and French, Brussels is the melting pot in the European Union, the seat of politics and numerous international companies making it the ideal environment for a girl seeking a new adventure in life to find her place. Everyone seemed to be in the same boat together. An expat community seeking refuge in their new adopted country, a place, like for so many others who came before, would become my home.

Chocolate, beer and waffles, there were so many reasons that Belgium made sense. Belgium seemed like the most unlikely places to end up, considering the array of options I had at my disposal. London, Sydney, Melbourne, Germany, Austria and Italy all had topped my list at one point or another since my childhood. My aunt Pam was someone I looked up to and adored from a very young age. She was like a big sister I never had. At 27 she moved to Texas, leaving the administrative work at a local refrigeration factory behind her to pursue a life in a "big" city. She settled in San Antonio where she fell in love with my uncle, an army man who had traveled the world. He would take her too on this journey across the continental US to Korea. She influenced my young mind in a way that my parents never could because she had the experience living and working outside of my small town.

Do you remember what you wanted to be or where you wanted to live when you were growing up? Well, luckily enough in this instance, my memory still served me. The practical side of me at one point wanted to be a hairdresser, all day every day styling clients' hair, but that moment passed. I never became the country music singer I wanted to either. It turns out I am not Dolly Parton, and my whimsical corals in the shower are the least likely to be heard center stage at the Grand Old Opry. I just don't have the voice for it, but many other things I had set my sights upon came to fruition and living in Europe was to be one of them.

Belgium I found is and was a bit of a mystery. When I began telling my friends of my impending move, they looked at me with wonder. Why Belgium? For many, Belgium was mistaken for a city in Germany. For them, it didn't even register Belgium is an actual country even though it houses all the major European Institutions, Parliament, the European Community and NATO. Others, friends, and acquaintances knew it was a country but couldn't quite identify it on a map.

So why Belgium exactly? Even the Belgians themselves couldn't understand my fondness for their country. Why on earth would I ever want to leave America, the home of the free and the land of the brave? It wasn't so simple. There were many contributing factors to my ultimate decision. First of all, I needed a change. Setting the dark chocolate nougat filled truffles aside for a moment.

I had accumulated a variety of friends located throughout the country. From Bruges where I had met Kyle, to Genk, in eastern Belgium, where I volunteered at an English youth camp, I had stopped over in Gent, a dynamic university town for a ten-day-long music festival before heading to Antwerp and finally making my way to Brussels. It was in this capital city where I had the largest network of support. Months into planning, I had reached out to one friend, specifically Justin, whom I knew would have a spare room available. His old roommate had moved out heading back to the United States, and he would not have a replacement for some time.

Predictions aside, I wasn't sure what he would say when I asked if I could impose on his apartment considering we had only met on a couple of occasions. I was a friend of a friend. Gambling on a long shot, what did I have to lose asking a simple question? I so often thought of life in this way. Be aggressive, thinking back to my high school days where I was cheerleading on the sidelines of a varsity football game rooting the offense down the field, B-E—A-G-G-R-E-S-S-I-V-E, my red and black pom-poms whirling in the air. What was the worst thing that could happen? It was merely a question. If I could handle what life had to throw at me then why not run straight at it? Justin could easily have said no, but with a kind heart and open arms, he agreed to my proposition. That is how my story began in Belgium.

Justin would play an indispensable role in making my transition a smooth one. You see, Justin is the life of the party. When he walks in the room the energy shifts. There is no way to explain it fully but to say he is a firecracker. Loud and flamboyant, he never ceased to amaze me. He is one of those likable types that gets along with almost everyone. Justin's colorful personality and quirky wit glistens through the clouds. He is someone that everyone wants to know, and I was fortunate to leech onto his reputation.

Okay, leeching sounds like I was desperate. I wasn't, but I was in a lucrative position to make friends and network with a very international, well-connected group of individuals whose networks transgressed not only Belgium but throughout Europe. That was one of my favorite aspects about Brussels and becoming an expat in particular. It was remarkable how small the world became once I stepped out into it. I had connections everywhere.

The proximity of countries made short weekend trips frequent and accessible. Easier than crossing state lines I could have breakfast in Germany, lunch in the Netherlands, pass back through Belgium and be under the Eiffel Tower in Paris before nightfall! Not to mention the cheap airlines that were only a click away. I could board a plane for the weekend and be transported seaside, enjoying the magnificent Mediterranean climate in two hours or less. Life was good.

Brussels a city of about 1.9 million residents which includes all the outlying suburbs is, in fact, small if you consider it the "capital" of Europe. Coming from Phoenix, where the population reaches 4.3 million citizens, not including the transient Hispanic population, doubles Brussels in size. What Brussels lacks in size it more than makes up for in heart. The city offered everything I imagined a European city would. History, architecture, infrastructure, open-air markets, tiny artisan shops, cobblestone streets and massive gilded buildings. The Grand Place, a short walk from the Central Railway Station, felt like a step back in time to the merchant guilds of the Middle Ages.

The beauty with Brussels was that it wasn't Paris or London. Yes, it had its good share of tourists, but it was a very livable city at the same time. If you wanted to steer clear from the crowd, you could. At the same time, because the city supported the institutions and the institutions supported the city, there were an incredible array or restaurants and bars, not to mention you could attend an event every night of the week. Being bored wasn't an option, and it wasn't long that I was making friends all on my own.

Once I arrived, I had a social life, but life was not one big party. Though how amazing it would be if it were. There finally came a point where I had to get serious. I had to come up with a concrete reason to stay. I needed a job to apply for temporary residency; otherwise, three months would pass, and the country I had so quickly fallen in love with would give me the boot and send me packing. Belgium, part of the Schengen, a group of countries within the European Union that signed a formal agreement with the United States allowed US citizens the right to stay within its borders for any given 90 days within a six-month period without a visa. If you wanted to surpass this allotted time period and work, a visa was required, and the authorities were not giving them away like cotton candy.

Language wasn't my strong suit. Generalizing the American population on a whole, I think we are underdeveloped in this area. Because most business in the world is conducted in English, there is really little to no motivation to tackle the challenge of learning another language outside of our mother tongue. Again, this is a really big generalization and not always the case. In Belgium, a country where there are three official national languages, French, Dutch and German, government, more importantly, immigration, was a bit challenging. This is modest and a bit of an understatement. Bureaucracy was primarily conducted in Dutch and French and, in some if not most offices, if you did not communicate in one of these languages then good luck progressing further. That was the first of many hurdles I had to overcome.

I had to find a liaison and fast. The clock was ticking. A good friend of mine living not far from where I was staying was Belgian. Her native language was Flemish, the Dutch language spoken in Flanders, and she also had a good comprehension of French, though she rarely spoke it. She would be my liaison in nearly all my correspondence with the local authorities. That was where it started, by just registering at the commune, or the town hall, the process began. They marked the day I entered Belgium and gave me a piece of paper telling me the date I would have to depart. That was my benchmark, three months. Whether I liked it or not that was all the time I had to convince the Belgian authorities to allow me to stay.

How did I do that exactly? Well, I come back to that calculated risk I speak so fondly about. Okay, I left Phoenix with two suitcases in hand, no job, no visa, no legitimate reason to stay. Unaware of the magic awaiting me - I leaped into the terrifying, dark chasm of uncertainty. What on earth was I doing? I thought as I faced a 10-meter-high brick wall of challenges I wanted to scale. What were the odds that I could contrive a valid reason? I wasn't blind nor ignorant, I knew what I signed up for, and I was up for it, though there is one thing that would make this feat even more trying.

My background is in hospitality, yes, over a decade of education and experience managing bars, restaurants and resorts, dealing with disgruntled diners and handling unruly men who want to either fight one another over petty squabbles or pinch your butt. I have dealt with both, and neither is appealing. On a happy note, I have orchestrated over a dozen weddings and secretly planned surprise engagements with nervous boyfriends wanting every last detail down to the flower petal to be perfect. I have been tossed around in a bar fight, bruising ribs when a confrontation between two men got out of hand at the end of the night. But it's not exciting. Hospitality can be boring, and sometimes it comes as a relief, spending late nights at the computer writing budgets, settling tills and being the glorified therapist when servers come to you with their personal problems. The industry is not glamorous, but in total, the high you get as the manager in the heat of the dinner rush is comparable to that of being the starring quarterback in the state football finals throwing the game-winning pass. Even though I had my share of ups and downs, I had a successful career, and it would make sense I would continue to pursue this field abroad, but I didn't. The change I so badly sought was a complete overhaul of my life.

In 2011, after four years of personal practice, I registered and trained to become a certified yoga instructor with two nationally recognized teachers, Jenn Chiraelli and John Salisbury. Three months after I graduated from ASU, I entered a different type of classroom that offered an array of new learning and spiritualty. From philosophy to alignment, I will forever be a lifelong student, and I saw teaching as an opportunity to give back, to help others the same way that it helped me in a way. Yoga was a gift I felt. The practice came to me in a time of personal struggle. Managing school, a full-time job and a relationship with Joshua that was hardly ever easy was demanding. I was losing weight because of stress and couldn't control my mind from running away with itself, mulling about homework one minute, work the next, what Joshua was doing, I couldn't put an end to the non-stop chatter. For the greater part of four years, I practiced three or four times a week, and I saw the impact it had on my life. I felt calm, with a clear mind and more compassion. Physically I was stronger than I had ever been and felt good in my skin. This had not always been the case. I always had issues with my body weight and appearance. Since I was in junior high I battled anorexia though I was never diagnosed with the eating disorder I knew I inflicted on myself.

I would go to school without eating breakfast and only drink orange juice for lunch. By the time I had a break at work after school it was 9 pm after the dinner rush where I may have had a lemon pepper chicken sandwich or a couple of mini pancakes with maple syrup. I needed the sugar to boost my energy levels so I could go home at the end of my shift and study before starting the cycle again. I battled with this affliction for over a decade. I weighed 95 pounds when I graduated from ASU with my Bachelor's degree in history. I was 25 years old, and I should have known better. I should have loved myself more.

Yoga teacher training offered tools to become aware of my problem and fully accept myself flaws and all. I still catch myself from time to time judging the reflection in the mirror by the number on the scale, but fortunately, the moment passes, and I come back to my learning.

By 2012, I had been teaching in local gyms and recreational centers but only on the side. It was never my main interest or source of income, and I wanted to see if I could reverse the roles. I wanted to flip my life upside down, to make black turn white and left turn right. To make yoga my primary interest and turn my passion for food and beverage into a therapeutic hobby. I wanted to find more balance, handing in the late nights and double shifts for Tibetan singing bowls and yoga mats.

Before leaving the United States I had contacted numerous yoga studios, spas and wellness centers in Brussels. Out of a dozen emails, I received three responses. One was scratched off the list right away; they said I had to be an independent contractor to work for them, which would be impossible as a foreigner. The two other messages were much more favorable. The answer wasn't a rejection letter but an invitation to discuss our options further. Being thousands of miles away didn't really allow us the ability to meet in person, but they said if and when I arrived in Belgium, they would be open to meeting. No assurance had been given, just the openness to the possibility of employment.

The first step of the process was complete, but what next? I would schedule meetings with both of these potential employers only to find out that the ideal scenario was exactly the same response I read via email months ago from the owners of the third yoga studio. I had read over research on the internet how to become an independent and asked around, but what I found from numerous sources was that it would be nearly impossible to apply for the independent contractor status as a foreigner not having European Union residency.

Okay, there are two ways to look at this situation. I just spent a thousand dollars to get to Belgium just to find out something that could have been explained via email. I could have let my frustration fester, but how would it have helped? This was a concrete hurdle obstructing my course. If I would accept this solution as a blanket statement, I would have tucked my tail between my legs and headed for home. Yes, it was unfavorable, but I would not accept defeat this early on and definitely not this easily. The other option, rather than admit failure, was to strike back, to make a concerted effort that if I did desert my cause, I would know there was no other choice. I needed to at least go through the process of applying for independent professional status in order to prove to these two potential employers that I was serious. I wanted to stay, and I would take every means necessary to figure out a way to do so.

I had to start at the beginning of the applications process. Getting online there were so many websites that provided information, primarily in French and Dutch. The language barrier didn't hold me back. If this was meant to be there would be someone along the way who would take pity or I would rather like to think would have a kind heart and help guide me in the right direction. My friends shuttled me here and there to various offices asking questions and identifying the documents I would need to present to the authorities. I had planned ahead; before I left the United States, I had prepared a file filled with all my pertinent information such as my birth certificate, college transcripts, identification cards, certifications, etc., but what I didn't have were fingerprints, an FBI background check and the original college diplomas from the institutions where I had studied.

In the big picture, it may have seemed like I had a lot of time on my hands. I didn't have a job or very much responsibility, but at the same time, everything was new to me. I had to scramble to get these materials within a particular time frame, having to send things priority mail over international waters and pay extra for rush transactions. Patience was key. There was no hastening the process with the FBI. They do things on their own time as you can imagine. I called once to confirm they received my request, but the person on the other end of the line was legally unable to confirm or deny they had my application in their possession and that was just how it was. Crossing my fingers, I prayed I would receive my records in time.

Looking back at it all now, I am so glad I went through all of the trouble. I had made copies upon copies of all the material the immigration authorities requested, and over time, I have used up these records. When you become an expat, it feels like all you do is file one form after another, a paper trail of your life from one country to the next.

Though the process felt long and drawn out, the relocation proceedings were enlightening. As children growing up in the tutelage of our parents and/or grandparents, we have the wisdom and expertise of these individuals in our corner, helping us and guiding us into adulthood. These people do not only shape our personalities and behaviors but also create a seamless transition. Over the years, by the time college graduation is upon your doorstep, you are a fully integrated, functioning adult who can contribute to society. When you enter a foreign country, it is like starting all over again, yet this time you are all on your own. You are not an adolescent teen, and your parents are not there to hold your hand and show you how it is done. Even if you call them, they are going to have no idea what you are talking about from taxes to opening a bank account, because they have never experienced that particular process in that specific country.

Two months had gone by since I entered Belgium, and I thought I had everything I needed, a thick file with a corresponding application in hand. I went to the social secretariat and was told frankly everything I presented wasn't enough. How could it not be enough, did they want a sample of my blood, maybe a note from the president?! This was the end of the road I thought. The reason so many expat sites and immigration agencies said applying for independent status was nearly impossible because it was. I was lacking one item and one item only, a national

ID number! I could not even obtain this item if I wanted to. It is like a social security number in the United States.

Game over, I had hit a dead end. It was time to pack up my things, or was it?

I went back to the potential employers, in a last-ditch effort to explain the predicament I was in. It was almost unheard of, but I had to try to convince the owners of the luxury spa that I would be a good investment in THEIR future. Looking at the two companies, the spa was the one that had the most potential, and I felt like they would be the likeliest to actually say yes. They were in need of another individual to help in the operations of their business, and they wanted to launch a yoga studio. Perfect! I had ample experience in managing restaurants that could be transferred to spa operations, and I had two and a half years of experience teaching yoga already under my belt not to mention the years of preparation that preceded becoming certified. I could be a tremendous asset if they chose to employ me.

What would stop them? I was giving the owners the answer to their impending problem. It wasn't that simple though. Belgium has many rules and regulations in favor of employees, which make employers hesitant to employ just anyone that applies. Business owners and managers want to make sure they have the right candidate making the interview process quite crucial. The amount of time and money that factor into the decision is especially significant. A business doesn't want to have a high turnover rate because that could potentially hinder the success of the operations over a period of time.

I had never been in this position before where I had to be my own biggest advocate. When I had to promote myself before, my resume and experience had spoken for itself. I had always had a good track record, longevity, trustworthiness, determination, motivation, not to mention I was easy to work with. I had a long-standing reputation for meeting and/or exceeding goals, working with budgets and managing staff.

In this small operation, there was more to it than just facts and numbers. The owners wanted to build the business, and that meant we had to also have a good understanding of our relationship and objectives. This was not a problem. I did not see myself moving back to the United States any time in the near future. I just got here, why would I be thinking about going back when I hadn't got what I wanted out of the experience in the first place? I felt like I would sign my life away for the chance to stay, and I nearly did.

When the day came to sign the contract written in French, I was hesitant. I needed to have a close friend who was Belgian read it to me and explain to me the articles outlined therein. It detailed what was expected of me, my roles and responsibilities, what qualified as infringements of the contract and the fines and penalties I would incur if I did something outside the contract to make the company look bad. Though it was very detailed, it all seemed fair and legit.

In the document, there were two articles that I was uncomfortable with, but I signed anyway. They were as stated: I would sign off on all my intellectual property as a yoga instructor and project manager. This was severe, as I only ever thought tech-savvy computer intellects and academic researchers had these limitations controlling ownership of their work. The other notable item was a non-compete clause. Perplexed, I thought why on earth you would put a non-compete clause on a yoga instructor? Well, three to six months would be rational. I guess a yoga instructor could be compared to a hairdresser leaving a salon. The company would want assurance the associate didn't take clientele with them at the end of their service, but this particular non-compete clause was austere. I was signing off in this formal agreement that when my employment was concluded that I could no longer work in the health and wellness industry within the country of Belgium for a period of eighteen months. This would mean I would have to lean back on my other profession in the foodservice industry or leave the country entirely to acquire employment thereafter.

As I mentioned before it was this or nothing. I could sign the contract which seemed all well and good outside the two articles previously mentioned, or I could start packing my bags. By this point, I had no other options. I, of course, had the best intentions that our working relationship would blossom and that I would stay with the company all the while I lived in Belgium. It was really the dream job, or at least I thought at the time. I had the responsibility for launching a yoga program without my own individual investment. I got the opportunity to witness the inner workings of a luxury day spa and work with a variety of specialists from around the world.

With the contract out of the way, I could begin applying for residency status in Belgium.

Meeting at a coffee shop in Brussels' North Railroad Terminal, one of the spa owners accompanied me to the immigration office that was tucked away on the second floor overlooking crowds of travelers and commuters with their briefcases in hand heading out into the city.

Standing there waiting, I could feel the energy shift under my feet. In a matter of minutes, I would hand off my file stuffed to the brim with my personal data, the accompanying contract and labor agreement to a clerk seated behind a desk in a stark white cubicle. After he was satisfied with the documents, we would be dismissed. Just like that, no pomp and circumstance. There was nothing more to do. From that point on, the file would be taken to the head of the Office of Foreign Affairs for the decision which could take up to three weeks.

Exiting the railway station, I felt a sense of relief interlaced with uncertainty. I had done everything in my power to get to this point, and all I could do now was hold my breath and wait.

WISDOM 1 IGNORE THE NAYSAYERS

In life, you will always have an array of cheerleaders rooting for you — family and friends — who believe in you no matter what. They know you will be successful and want to be there to revel in it when you are. However, there will also be negative people in your circles that will, out of spite or naivety, tell you why you will fail.

You know the type, those individuals that you come into contact with that don't have anything nice to say. They challenge your beliefs, aspirations and dreams and only serve to hold you back. While they may not always try to bring you down, they definitely do not motivate you to move forward.

Don't let them deter you from greatness.

Whether it is out of fear or jealously that you are daring to change your life, there will be people along the way that will try to steer you off your path. When you find yourself brooding around in your mind when things are not quite working out or going slower than expected, it will be easy to agree with the negative chatter that has cast its shadow, but try to shake the doubt and skepticism and reassert your confidence and determination.

If you notice you have accumulated friends that could be classified as "naysayers," part ways. You will have enough internal dialogue trying to dissuade you, there is no need for added commentary.

This again is not easy. Some of these individuals may have played a major role in your life but have only served to control and hold you stagnant. It will take courage and resolve to break old relationships and build healthy boundaries. It is like looking at a bad habit, knowing it is no good, but continuing to pursue it.

Take your time and reprogram yourself; identify with what behavior is acceptable and what is intolerable. Make strides to implement this awareness into practice and foster more good vibes and wholesome relationships in your life.

CHAPTER 10

LESSONS IN MAGIC

**"Magic is believing in yourself. If you can do that, you
can make anything happen."
-Johann Wolfgang von Goethe**

Balancing on the back edge of the board, I was ready for
the rush, an exhilarating descent out over the fresh blanket
of snow that covered the French Alps. I could see clouds
of billowing smoke coming from chimneys with steeply
slanted roofs dotting the foot of the mountain in a town
called Flaine. Just minutes from the Italian border, Mount
Blanc stood out in the distance high above the clouds, like
a gorgeous woman that can't but help draw attention in a
crowd. It was Easter morning, and the radiant rays of
sunlight made the dismal rain that had plagued our
previous days seem like a far, distant memory.

I was up here on my own, well, not exactly. It was my
idea, yes, but I had also convinced two of my good friends
to road trip from Brussels over the long holiday weekend.
We made the eight-hour jaunt north to south through
Germany, in and out of Switzerland to this secluded
winter wonderland. Joining me were avid snowboarders,
Americans stationed in Brussels with the military. They
worked in support of NATO (North Atlantic Treaty
Organization). I had met them, friends of the group of

guys I'd first made contact with in Bruges. I'd become aware of a whole contingent of American military personnel working active duty in Belgium in various capacities, from NATO to the US Embassy. SHAPE (Supreme Headquarters Allied Powers Europe) is the highest military headquarters with Allied Command Europe (ACE) near Mons a forty-five-mile drive from Brussels. Home to 16 national allies, the international staff, consisting of American military and civilian personnel help plan and coordinate the military deployment of NATO forces.

Meeting a group of American soldiers at a beer tasting in Bruges at the outset of my five-month journey of self-discovery after Joshua was random, but even more profound was the effect this chance meeting had on my overall integration in Belgium. This network of friends was that little piece of home, which gave me a sense of grounding in a personal moment of instability.

Awkward, a complete beginner still, it took me longer to do everything. Falling time and time again, I slowly edged my way down the mountain. I was holding up the party. It was evident they had more experience having grown up blazing down the trails in the Colorado Rockies and the Snowshoe Mountains of West Virginia. No match to their speed and agility, I dawned the white flag. I loved facing fears and still do, but it was another thing to feel a pressure to perform when I wasn't prepared. Trying to replicate their stunts and maneuvers, I would have needed a stretcher and the Red Cross to escort me down from the top of the mountain. I could do without an emergency visit to the ER, and I kind of liked it the way it was, alone, free to go at my own pace.

Like a bluebird out of its cage, I felt solitary in flight. After submitting my application at the Office for

Foreigners in Brussels, we'd packed up my friend's 4x4 Subaru with snow gear, a guitar, snacks and a camera before we hit the road. It was a late Friday afternoon, and nothing stood in our way between the city and the great outdoors. An eight-hour drive through France, into Switzerland, up a winding mountain road and back down again, we reached the northern border of Italy in the South of France at midnight. The street lights vanished into the tree-lined mountainside as we started our ascent to our cabin in the woods.

Under the moonlight, we pulled into the parking lot filled with cars with various license plates from all over Europe. We checked into our shared room, a very sparsely furnished flat with only the bare necessities. No big deal, it would only serve as a place to rest our heads and weary bodies after a long day of sport, any other luxuries would have been wasted on us. The fresh mountain air, aromas of pine and timber crept through the cracks in the window sill. Raindrops, a light sprinkle made little indents in the snow that lined the window ledge. We had arrived and stepped back in time to a life of a much simpler reality.

Nestling under the covers warm in my bed, I felt an overwhelming sense of tranquility blanket my body. The night beckoned as I closed my eyes and slowly drifted off into fairy tales, a dreamland of snowflakes falling in a winter utopia.

Standing atop the mountain was exactly what I needed. Overlooking the valley below I could see eager skiers and snowboarders alike moving from here to there like bees buzzing around a honey pot, a whole system of lifts that ascended the mountain to various stations. The little village below was vibrant and full of life. I could see for miles and stood there alone lost in my thoughts. From the present, from that very spot, I could look back on the past and see why things happened the way they did. In hindsight, I could now cherish the intense lows because they propelled me to unthinkable highs. I would never have imagined my life before would have led me to this.

Four months before, I was learning how to snowboard with Stephen in the Rocky Mountains, and now I was cutting through mounds of powdery white stuff in the Haute Savoie region of the French Alps, a part of the Grand Massif domain. To say I was anything less than tremendously lucky would be an understatement. Looking up to the blue sky, I whispered thank you. Life has an amazing way of working out. It places you in the right place at the right time, not always knowing why exactly or understanding fully why you, among all people, were selected to receive such a wonderful gift.

I had met amazing people, traveled to more places than I had ever been before, and freed myself from the limitations I had once placed on myself. I learned to love myself completely, not allowing internal dialogue to be destructive and stepping up to the challenge when the odds were not on my side. My future had once been written for me, and now I had the power within myself to edit the outcome.

Preparing for change and going through the actual motions are two very different things. Reality sets in, and things may not go exactly to plan. The trick to navigating this period of uncertainty is to float like a feather in the wind, to move gracefully and adapt to the volatility and motion that will accompany the ride.

Ten days after getting back from my so-called "winter holiday" in the French Alps I received a call from my employer saying she had been notified by the Department of Foreign Affairs that she could come to pick up my work permit. I WAS APPROVED! A country not credited for being very timely in government affairs, Belgium seemingly amazed not only me personally but my friends as well who had become accustomed to the unhurried sense of urgency that is predominant in many European countries. Now that I have lived in Belgium, studied in Italy and worked in England, I think it is a fair statement. I was utterly floored not only by the speed but by the outcome. I didn't know what to say. I was speechless, and that rarely happens. Everyone dreams of a happy-ever-after, but I was actually taking part in it. I was the princess in my own fairy tale.

I had plans B, C and D tucked away in my back pocket all along. If needed, I could have escaped to Croatia hiding out on Kevin's sailboat all the while licking my wounds becoming Captain Hook or a distressed sailor. Not a bad idea, but not the ideal recourse. I could have found solace in a remote corner of India, digging deeper into my yoga study or thrown caution through the window and moved to Australia. It turned out I didn't need to reach into my reserve treasure trove of magnificent dreams when the first shot was right on target.

Now I had to get a handle of the logistics. It seemed outlandish at the time, but it was a requirement. There was no way to get around it, I had to actually return to the

United States, to the region of my last residence, Phoenix, and apply at the consulate in that geographic location which turned out to be Los Angeles, a six-hour drive away from the Phoenix Valley.

It wasn't the ideal scenario having to buy an international flight last minute just to return and submit a file and wait yet again. Immigration is a process of hurry up and wait, and there is nothing to do but accept the procedure with infinite patience and persistence. Of course, the authorities couldn't give me the exact amount of time in which this process would happen. Why would I expect any other response? They could only tell me applying for a Belgian visa could take anywhere from one to three weeks to be finalized. International flights are expensive in general, but last minute they're even worse.

On the bright side, there is always a bright side I could fly into Phoenix and make the reasonably short drive to Los Angeles and file my paperwork. I could then return to Phoenix, to friends and take care of any last details I hadn't handled before my earlier departure when I embarked on this feat. I now knew this was a definitive move. I wouldn't be returning to the United States for the foreseeable future, or at least I wasn't planning to. Anything that needed my personal attention would have to be handled in the short period that was allotted. Perfect and so a plan was set!

I had visited Los Angeles on a few occasions, and this trip was not out of the ordinary except that I was on a mission to quickly drop off my visa paperwork at the Belgian Consulate. A tedious task, yes, but it was a good excuse to hit the highway and get the heck out of the desert heat. I landed in the valley as the cusp of summer was looming overhead and the brutal dry heat of the desert landscape, which can only be compared to sticking your head into an oven set for roasting a ham, had already started to settle in. Initially, I planned on hopping a budget flight that would fly me in and out of Los Angeles in a day, but considering this was a last-minute arrangement, the budget airliner was no cheaper than flying halfway across the country.

Considering my options, I was online one afternoon in Brussels, a week before my flight back to the States. I was toying with the idea of renting a car and making the six-hour drive from the outskirts of Phoenix into downtown LA myself. While I was on my computer, my old roommate Brent appeared on one of my social feeds, and I wondered what he had been up to. We were always very close. He had moved into a two-bedroom apartment I had rented with another girl that didn't work out because of a clash in personalities. His moving in was a blessing. After the previous roommate situation, I needed some structure in my life, and he was perfect to fit the role. More like siblings than just friends, he was like a younger brother. We would hang out on a Saturday morning having coffee on our terrace overlooking the manicured apartment grounds or go out for beers downtown at a local microbrewery. His family was close and had invited me to join in their Thanksgiving celebrations when I couldn't make it home to Iowa to be with my own.

Since his lifestyle was flexible based on his occupation and spontaneity wasn't foreign to him, he was the perfect candidate. He was a west coast guy who relished doing things last minute or off the edge. Brent would be my co-pilot and partner in crime on a 24-hour rendezvous to the beach and back with a little business thrown in on the side.

It had only been a few days after I stepped foot on American soil and was nearly acclimated to the 100-degree heatwave when we set out destination Venice Beach. In no time we were on interstate I-10 in a black 4x4 Jeep Wrangler I had rented at the airport. I was back in the land of the free and the home of excessively large vehicles. We were West Coast bound, tunes blaring and sun in our eyes. I was "California Dreaming," thinking this is what memories are made of. It is not always the big picture moments, but the little experiences that add up to a life well-lived.

Before we left Phoenix, I asked Brent what was the one thing he had never done before and wanted to do? One of my friends I'd met years ago in an old monastery converted to a youth hostel had shown me his ink, a tattoo that read clearly, "Why not?" He was an American straight out of high school when we met backpacking through Europe. He explained that he and thirteen other friends he'd made in Prague decided one night to all get the same tattoo placed above their ankle. It served as a reminder to always ask, "why not?" Of course, and more importantly, I think a great question is, "What's the worst that could happen?"

I loved this idea of incorporating something I had never done before into this trip. I didn't want to just drive to Los Angeles, I wanted to create a daring adventure. Responding to my question, Brent, quite sure of himself said, well, "Why not sleep on the beach?" I thought to myself, hmmm...why didn't I think of that? Simple enough, why had I never done it myself? What was the worst that could happen?

Los Angeles is one of those cities that is, for me at least, a culinary treat. I had always thought of it as the arm-pit of American cities stinky and plastic, everyone wanting to be someone else in a materialistic jungle of fancy cars and million-dollar houses nestled next to gang violence and poverty. It wasn't until I took a three-day trip to the city in February 2012 to meet my friend David, who was passing through the United States on his way from Panama City back home to Melbourne, that I fell in love. The art, culture, weather, the diversity, the city has it all and more. From the LA County Art Museum where we wandered the galleries and took in an old black and white indie film in the museum's massive auditorium to walking the Santa Monica Pier, we canvassed the city like tourists with a keen eye for the eclectic. We walked from Beverly Hills to Melrose Avenue where we bought one of a kind designer sneakers that I felt were more of a collector's piece than an accessible fashion statement. David was into street art, capturing images with his photographic lens later to be enlarged and put on display. That was when I started to get into graffiti, looking at it less as vandalism but more as a valid form of artistic expression.

Outside of the art and fashion scene, we explored many restaurants and the places I still patronize such as Taste and Marino Restaurante on Melrose, the Figtree Café on the Venice Beach boardwalk or a little further walk to Poke Poke and my favorite Gjelina. When it comes to tasty creations, LA does not lack in innovative fare.

Cutting it close, it was almost midnight when we strolled up to this little gem in the heart of Venice. Getting there near closing time was actually a blessing as we could thwart the crowds of tourists and locals who were a constant fixture in this part of town. Sitting in the dimly lit dining room, the candles cast shadows of patrons on the stained concrete walls. We enjoyed a sumptuous bottle of red wine from the Russian River Valley and nibbled on delectable bites. Watching on as a collection of chefs gathered in the small square prep space in the center of the room, diners sipped their shaken martinis and conversed softly.

Sitting in such comfort, my roommate and I were toiling over his proposal, the idea of rejecting the obvious normal means of accommodation for the unconventional. The beach had an uncanny appeal. Knowing that it would be frowned upon by our parents or any other "normal" member of society made it all the more seductive. Yes, I know it sounds crazy, right, but I think by now, crazy had a welcome place in my vocabulary!

I come back to calculated risk. I like to say why not, but here are the facts. One, there are a lot of bums that call the boardwalk on Venice Beach their permanent residence. The weather is sublime, and the public toilets have showers. Life could, of course, be better for the less fortunate, but it wasn't a horrible predicament. Hold on a second, did I forget to mention that medical marijuana is pretty easy to get your hands on? That was something we were not in want of as Brent had brought his own personal supply from home. I feel fairly well equipped to say that the bums that call Venice Beach home are some of the friendliest I have met in all of my travels, tan-skinned and high as a kite. The only thing is it's not very advisable for you to sleep on the beach yourself.

We were still not sure about our accommodation for the evening. A couple of fairly clean-cut middle-class individuals didn't really fit the ideal image of freeloading hippies wandering about. Looking out of place was the least of our worries, but what was more important neither one of us really checked the weather forecast before embarking on this journey. Ocean breezes that felt refreshing under the blaze of the radiant sun are very different from those that sting in the cold damp sand under the glow of the moon. Rather than sleep on the beach without cover we resolved to the next best thing, sleeping in the jeep facing the coast so that the first thing we would awake to would be the waves rolling in as the Pacific Ocean unveiled its grandeur in the dawning moments of the soft morning light. We were not the only ones with this fabulous idea, there were multiple cars parked in this manner when we rolled into our parking space facing the Pacific.

As the dawn approached, we tossed and turned and woke to the calm tides crashing on the sand. Nothing could be better than grabbing a cup of coffee at my favorite morning hangout, a beachside bar with California cuisine, fresh and local, listening to the strumming of a guitar by an artist earning his keep. I freshened up in the restaurant bathroom. When I returned to the table, there was no evidence that I had just woken up from a passenger seat.

The sky was a hazy gray as crisp ocean breezes made their way across the sand. The waiter brought our breakfast to the table, homemade scones and marmalade, a veggie omelet served with guacamole and fresh mango salsa.

Good morning, California, oh how I have missed you! Have you ever noticed there are certain places and people in your life that you return to time and time again, the love you share never wavers no matter the time you have spent apart? Well, this is the relationship I have with California; it never ceases to please. I could live a lifetime away only to return to her warm embrace.

Before enjoying our day, we had one task and one task only. My mission was to drop off my visa application at the Belgian Consulate's office. Even to this day, it astounds me that I was forced to return to the Belgian

Consulate in the Southwest region, a nine-hour flight and six-hour drive from Brussels, Belgium, for what turned out to be a ten-minute appointment. I presented my life in an organized file of papers, as I had done before. I was becoming a pro. I handed over my passport and work permit and finally took a 'glamorous' headshot for the visa. Of course, it was not my best look, from sleeping in a car to a government-issued ID. Everything said and done, we were in and out lying on the beach within the hour, soaking up the rays of the beautiful West Coast light.

As we pulled up to the coast we had a lightbulb moment, to ride a tandem bicycle down the Venice Beach boardwalk. Surprisingly enough, I had never ridden a bike tandem, and I actually felt a bit afraid of enduring physical pain. The type that can bloody the knees and possibly even break bones. The thought of taking down not only myself but the both of us on this contraption was terrifying, not to mention the crowds of onlookers or innocent bystanders. It sounds silly, but bicycling is not a forte of mine. The big question was who should steer? I would rather be the hopeless victim in the back rather than take the reins navigating through the pedestrian jungle.

Before we ventured out on the pavement with the bike, we hit the beach to catch up on some much-needed rest from the night before. Sleeping in a car did not conform to the comforts of a hotel room, and we both looked like we had seen a better day. A little rough around the edges, we dozed off under the sun listening to the therapeutic sounds of the rolling waves. The air was sweet, and the day was ours. Losing track of time, we awoke to realize we looked like fried tomatoes left out on the vine for a bit too long. Sand all over and a little crisp, we bellied up to a seaside cabana and rather than make a mockery of ourselves riding a bicycle we opted for a plate of fish tacos washed down with the quintessential salted margarita. Two things that are not abundant in Belgium.

Winding down the day, the sun was about to disappear under the horizon as we set the cruise control Phoenix bound. In 24 hours, we experienced what some take for granted. It didn't matter we had so little time, but it was the quality of the time we shared.

Brent opened my eyes and affirmed a question that lingered in the back of my mind since I had left in January. Did I have any true friends in this place I once called home? I did. After not having spoken for a little over three months, it felt like we had come out of hibernation and the season never changed. It wasn't that way with everyone though. It takes time to weed a garden, to get rid of what is not adding beauty to the landscape and to find out what blossoms you cannot live without. I discovered some friendships were not meant to be nurtured and that the roots were not very deep, making it easy to move on to those roses not yet in full bloom.

Getting back to Phoenix, I still had to wait. I had to visit my storage unit, meet with the bank and tidy up all the loose ends I had left undone. Moving is wonderful, a fresh start, a new beginning out there somewhere. Some people can drop their life and pick it up on the other side of the globe like it is no big deal, but for the majority, it is a little more consuming than that. If you have no attachments or wants in regard to worldly possessions, then nothing is holding you back from seeking your paradise, but typically it is not so easy.

For the rest of us moving across the continental United States may sound fabulous, but in reality, it is stressful, hiring a moving van, maybe some guys to pack up your things or maybe you opt to do the heavy lifting yourself. Placing all your belongings into cardboard boxes only to be delivered, unpacked and put in its place in a home so far away. Add an ocean to that equation, and you may as well start from scratch when it comes to packing up the house.

I retained a small storage unit in the United States for about four years after my move. I don't know why exactly, maybe it was the memories, the pictures, the books, my cooking supplies that I couldn't let go of. Someday I thought I would treat it like Christmas morning, where wild-eyed children tear open the presents Santa Claus left under the tree. I thought I would eventually return to unlock my unit and find all the wonderful things I thought were of value waiting for my return. I wondered by the time that day came if any of the things that had remained would have had the same meaning as before. I had lived so long without the contents that going into these boxed memories seemed unnecessary. I learned the art that less-is-more and these objects held no more significance than a Styrofoam cup of coffee, easily recycled without a second thought.

When it came time to start setting up house in Belgium, I wasn't all too fond of the idea of ordering a shipping crate and having my things transported to Europe. The expense, the management of these affairs, I just didn't want to tackle the enormity of the acquisition if I didn't have to be bothered. At this point, I still didn't know what my future would hold. Though things were starting to become more definitive, there was still a hint of the unknown. I had a one-year contract, and after that year, I could be anywhere. My employer did not have to renew my contract, nor did I have to agree to the conditions and continue my employment if it were not going well. One year, five years, there was still a cloud of ambiguity that lingered overhead, but there was a glimmer of light shining through.

With that long-winded explanation, I decided to forego retrieving the last of my belongings when I moved into my bright, open 35-meter square apartment on the second floor of a newly remodeled four-story building that housed a cleaning company on the street level. A one-bedroom flat with an open kitchen located two blocks from Place Chatelain, where a popular open-air market was held every Wednesday afternoon. A place all the expats and members of the EU institutions would gravitate to network and socialize after work. I liked the shopping, and of course, the ability to have a glass of champagne while buying my produce wasn't a bad deal either.

Not but a short walk from work, this trendy residential area in Brussels was welcoming. I wheeled in my two suitcases and decided it was time to go furniture shopping. I was starting a whole new life, and why not recreate it entirely from the ground up? It wouldn't take much, going from my spacious apartment in the United States to what felt like a college dorm or a walk-in closet would only take the bare necessities, a couch, a table and chairs that would accompany the bed and drawers I had already acquired at IKEA. Within two weeks, I was entertaining my first house guests. Making new memories in a place I would now call home.

WISDOM I PATIENCE & PERSISTENCE

My Grandma Barb once reminded me, "patience is a virtue, darling." Rarely was she a passenger in my car, but when she was, I think my driving habits made her a bit edgy, maneuvering in and out of traffic. She said I was just like my grandfather, always in a rush.

The difference between success and failure is patience and persistence. It is irrational to think that success is achieved overnight, rather, it takes time and that, my friend, is why you need patience. In the face of challenges and setbacks, hiccups or detours, blockades on the road to greatness, it takes persistence to see anything, big or small, through to fruition.

To succeed, you need both patience and persistence. Patience is important; on its own, it means the ability to tolerate time or a particular way of being. Patience is wisdom. It is the ability to sit back in an old rocking chair and watch life flow organically without pushing or pulling, trying to control the outcome. Finding the balance between patience and persistence is key. You can have all the patience in the world, but without persistence, you will end up nowhere. Persistence is the drive needed to see an objective through, to meet every challenge and rejection and consistently push back not accepting failure or defeat. Without persistence, patience on its own may never achieve a thing.

In times of great change, it is important to be flexible, to know when to stress, to step in and fight and when it is more effective to just throw your hands in the air, to breathe and let life unfold.

Having patience and persistence is a practice. Begin with yourself. Having patience with yourself will lead you to be more understanding and patient with those that surround you.

Persistence gives patience an intention. If there isn't a goal or purpose in which you are applying yourself to, what can seem like patience is really dawdling.

Find your purpose, and patience and persistence will guide you to see it through with ease.

CHAPTER 11

THE TRUTH WITHIN

"What lies behind us and what lies before us are tiny matters compared to what lies within us."
–Ralph Waldo Emerson

In Brussels, I surrounded myself with a few locals and a majority of expats. It was a fair balance considering my background and my limited language acumen. Integrating into society, I signed up for French courses, but I was far from fluent. Because the city was so reliant upon expats, rather than being in the minority, I was actually in the majority. When it came to language, English was what everyone used primarily in international circles to communicate. Out of any European city on the continent, this remark excludes Great Britain and Ireland. Brussels was my match. The country offered a smooth transition from the American way of life to a more European lifestyle coasting on the high of politics and legislature. It was like living in Washington D.C. without the White House.

What was fascinating about Brussels and what I learned straight away was the spirit and drive to be an entrepreneur, to get out there in the crowd and make a name for yourself. If you don't learn that quickly, you will be lost in the hustle and bustle.

I was single when I moved to Belgium, and that made things easier. Not to say that having a partner, a companion to come home to would not have been nice, it would have been a welcomed addition. It would have helped to have that person there to reassure me the gamble was paying off even if loneliness and unease crept into the recesses of my mind and held me captive at night falling asleep alone.

Being single allowed me to focus on my career. I had not only changed the place I called home, but I also delved into the world of health and wellness when all I had ever known before was food and beverage.

At first, I felt like I could move at a more relaxed pace. I had more consistency in my life, and I loved the structure. I had specific times to be on the clock, and other times, I could unwind with friends and go to the movies or sit in the park reading a book. I felt this sense of ease that work was complimentary to my social life and not the primary focus, a change from the mentality I had become accustomed to back in the United States where work came first, and extra-curricular activities were packed in the day only if they fit in the cracks. One of my favorite memories was road-tripping to a small city in the Flanders region to go to a Dropkick Murphy's concert with some of the security staff from the US Army Garrison. It was a big industrial storage building converted into a roughneck concert hall in what felt like a timeworn manufacturing town. I tagged along, like a little sister, my brothers were there to guard and protect. Elbowing our way to the front of the crowd, my friends ushered me over the metal guard barrier and onto the stage. I was enamored with delight as others too were hoisted up with the band, where we sang their final song "I'm Shipping Up to Boston," and had the opportunity to talk to the band after the performance. What a fabulous experience!

I found that businesses operated by Belgian natives did not often question tradition. It was hard to paint a picture outside the constraints they had limited themselves to. What had worked before would continue to work, there was no reason to rewrite the script. This was very apparent in brewing where brewers relied on time tested recipes from generations long ago creating a quality product without any impurities. This habit of conforming to tradition worked for both the product and service industries. If you came in with a new, bright idea, it would be hard to convince the manager or CEO that this new, untested concept would improve business when there was a track record of perceived success from before.

How does that relate to my new career in health and wellness? I was hired to not only act as a project manager, organizing and executing events and workshops, filling in as staff at the spa, but I was also given the task to launch a new yoga studio. The owners were not Belgian, and they did not concede to this dated ideal of lingering in the past, unhurried to the call for action. They were progressive, thinking outside the box and had an enthusiastic drive to create greatness.

I learned a lot over the first few months, and I enjoyed the challenge. I didn't speak French, but the owners had accounted for this. I worked with a staff rich in many languages from all over Europe and Asia. Everyone was from somewhere, and we worked together cohesively, helping one another where needed. French lessons were a must and, once again, I became a student, a status I was very comfortable with. Bringing my background into play, I helped to restructure their training program, revitalize the inventory control and aid in overall service. A few months into my employment, a space became available next to the spa that would create the ideal environment for the yoga studio, and we started to work on that project. Over the course of the year, I had my hands in on nearly every aspect of operations outside of giving massages myself, though I was grateful to receive my fair share, one of the many perks derived from training and honing beautiful talents. Though I enjoyed learning the operations side of running a luxury spa and I felt it was applicable to my career, I got the most pleasure from building relationships with my students and seeing them progress in their practice and in their lives. It was rewarding to know I was making an impact on their health and wellness.

At first, I had found a balance between my personal and professional life. I felt my time was respected, but as the honeymoon period passed, the line that separated the two got muddled, and I felt like I was on call 24/7. Of course, management did not see it this way. They made it clear I could define my own schedule based upon the classes I taught, the clients I saw, and the hours I worked in the spa, but even outside of work I was engaged in networking events where the topic of my conversation was the promotion of the spa. It never ended. I had started working for the spa before I even had a contract in hand, giving private lessons and making plans for the new space. By the time I joined the team and we were fully functioning, I was teaching close to 18-20 hours of yoga per week in addition to my daily tasks at the spa. This may not sound like much, but you add in administrative duties in conjunction to giving classes and creating promotions, workshops, events, two shifts handling the front desk concierge duties, managing inventory and ordering and I felt I had more than a full plate of responsibilities sitting before me. What I had so hoped to find, that balance I was trying to achieve was lost, and I did not see it coming back in the near future as we progressed making bigger goals and setting new ambitions to expand our operations to other international cities.

In regard to the business that seemed all well and good. I felt like if the business was a success, I had done my job. Students were starting to increasingly flock to our humble nest, creating a sacred space where everyone felt safe to grow in both their physical and spiritual yoga practices. The spa was already an established haven of wellness in the city. We were on the fast track toward stardom, but I felt I wasn't getting what I wanted out of the experience. I wasn't being fulfilled. At some point, I pushed the button into autopilot, and the roles I filled became redundant. We were trying to grow our yoga community, but I was the only instructor for the first six months. I had no one else to feed off or offer inspiration or insight. Yes, I was learning things along the way about social media and marketing, but for the most part, I felt like I was leading a start-up that was not my own with very little involvement of the management, and that was not what I had signed up for. I look back, and I could have coasted through one more year as it was, but the turning point came when I was asked to contribute to a wellness book the spa was writing around Christmas time. Nearly three months until my contract would be up for renewal and I was asked to contribute content. As the token chef, nutritionist and yoga/meditation instructor in the spa, I would hold the weight of the pen. Where else would they accumulate this information from recipes to yoga sequencing? The massage therapists were not qualified for such a task. They could contribute practical tools to aid in de-stressing and relaxation, but I felt my work would comprise the majority of pages between the covers.

When I asked how I would be recognized for my contribution, I was told the only recognition I would receive was an article stating the spa staff contributed to the material. The "staff," my name would never be referenced? While I understand the concept of ghostwriting; this was not for me. I was told my intellectual property was owned by the spa, and my signature relinquished my rights in my employment contract. I was enraged and frankly angry at myself for not seeing it sooner. Relationship, what working relationship did we have? I was just another peg in the wheel that went around. What outraged me most, and I felt entitled to contend with was that I never signed off my intellectual property as a chef, I was never hired on as such. Any nutrition advice or recipes would remain at my discretion.

The owners were intuitive and felt my rising frustration. Our friendship and our working relationship suffered. The book was never written. The owners invited me to London, in addition to two other supervisors at the spa, for a wellness conference. I sensed they were trying to make amends and reaffirm they valued my presence on the team, but it was too late. My feelings had been hurt, and I felt like I had been belittled. That was in January, and it wasn't until March when the time came to discuss the renewal of my contract that my exasperation was addressed.

The owners were the ones that came to my aid. In a time of uncertainty, they offered me a place at their table, on their team, and yes, I was very grateful. I had fond memories with both the staff and clients from organizing Wine and Canvas art events to VIP Holiday Sales Bazaars.

We shared many successes, but over the year I always felt there was this little voice inside me telling me that the only reason I was in the position I was in Belgium was because the owners took a risk and, at any moment, all that I had worked so hard to create would be taken from me. I always felt that I owed them more than the rest. There was a higher expectation for me to perform. I was constantly reminded that I was a financial burden and what financial figure we needed to meet at the end of the month to make their expenditure on me make sense for the business.

The only thing that got me through the last three months were my yoga students. They were that little sparkle of light in the dark of night that made everything right in my day. I knew I couldn't go on like this caring about one aspect of my job and feeling as though I was turning on autopilot in other areas of the business. My overall happiness was diminishing. I needed to start contemplating my future.

What were my options? If I wanted to stay in Belgium, which I did, I could either find another company to work for or go independent. Remember that was what I was trying to become from the beginning, a professional contractor, an independent, as it is referred to? The missing link had been secured. What was lacking before was a Belgian identification number, and now that I had a work permit in my possession, I also had an ID number.

This decision was not one that I took lightly. I was told very early on that with becoming independent came much more responsibility. Taxes, social securities, everything with owning your own business would rest on my shoulders. Even if I was one individual person, I would still be considered a business entity. Time had come to start investing my energies into myself rather than diverting them towards someone else's dream. I could either go on like this wishing away my days for a brighter tomorrow, hoping things would get better or I could take charge of my own life. I was on the cusp of making a breakthrough.

It was a Friday late in the afternoon when I was sitting in my office in the basement of the yoga studio with one of my colleagues, Nevena. Sitting across from one another at our small square conference table, we took a break from staring into our computer screens. I asked her what her plans were for the evening. Nevena replied she had nothing special in mind but thought she would just stay in for a quiet evening. She'd had a hectic week preparing for a fundraising event and could use some much-needed rest and relaxation curled up at home with a good book and a glass of wine.

I approached her with an idea of going to some posh club I had just heard about called Jeux D'Hiver. There was a big winter celebration many of my expat friends were going to, and I thought it would be fun to do something different for a change. I'm not sure what quite got into me as clubbing was not my thing, but recently I had been acting peculiar. It had all started when I had finally filed my application for independent status. I had this urge to step outside of my comfort zone. I felt poised and confident, and it made me want to be out in the crowd and in the limelight. It was okay that Nevena didn't want to join. I had two or three other activities, from tapas with a friend to a low-key house party I was also wagering so I thought I would figure it out on a whim. Whatever sounded the most appealing when I was getting ready for the night out would win.

I decided to go to dinner, meet up with some others at the house party, and ultimately head to the club with friends that would pick me up on their way. This was really unlike me. I would have been happy just going to the movies and calling it an early night as I had to teach yoga the next morning bright and early which is not congruent with dancing to dawn. But I pulled on a champagne-colored cocktail dress with a dipping neckline and black leather pumps anyway, hair curled, I added the finishing touches to my makeup, and at five minutes to eight, I was out the door and off to the first of my engagements. I was meeting a dear friend of mine for dinner at a little, bustling tapas bar around the corner that was a charming local hangout near Place Chatelain, where all the trendy bars and restaurants were.

Wining and dining, I made my way to the house party in just enough time to meet everyone, say my hellos, kissing one another on the cheek (I was pretty European by now.) We packed in a couple cars, parked at the entrance to the forest and made our way down a small path in the woods. The club was very secluded, a stylish place to go and be seen. Women dressed in their finest cocktail attire, from short sequined dresses to tight black lace ensembles, there was no expense spared. I could probably count on my two hands the number of times I had been clubbing in my life, not to mention the rare occasion it had been in Belgium. Feeling a little awkward, I was out of my element. A couple of glasses of bubbles in addition to the red wine I had with dinner, I quickly fell in tune with the group I was with. Everyone knew one another and was out to have a fabulous time dancing the night away.

From the middle of the crowded room, I caught his eye. As he came closer, I played it off that I hadn't noticed him at all until he was right next to me. He was in a line of people walking from one side of the dance floor to the other. Twisting and turning, I let go of my inhibitions. I pulled him aside, and we started to dance. Our bodies touching, his hands caressed my lower back; I was having such an amazing time that I forgot he was a complete stranger. When the song stopped, he escorted me outside onto the terrace flanked by two fire pits to talk and warm our hands under the stars. He was attractive, a square jawline, dark hair swept back, wearing a tan blazer over a starched white button-up, tailored jeans and Italian leather shoes, everything about him was speaking to my senses. I was drawn into his deep brown eyes, and I could hardly resist myself.

Making small talk, I tried to gain my composure. I had spoken to other men that night, but no one had this effect on me. I can't lie, I had the nerve to pull him on the dance floor, to fondle this strange man like he was my own, but now I was at a loss as to what to say or where to go next. I wanted to hand over the reins and let him lead, but he was congenial and restrained. The evening was starting to catch up to me, maybe one champagne too many. I was tired. I wasn't the type to go home with a complete and total stranger or take a courtesy ride, not knowing where it could lead. I had been spontaneous before with nothing to avail. I kindly excused myself. Leaving only my name as a glass slipper, I dashed out into the night.

My watch read five in the morning as I got into the back of the taxi cab. I would only have a few hours to recuperate before teaching my first class. When I arrived at my apartment, I checked my voice messages as I always tend to do. Being abroad, I hardly ever got phone calls from my family and friends, but on this early morning, I was surprised by a familiar voice on the other end of the line. Just before dawn, I listened to my brother tell me there was a very troubling situation at home. My aunt Pam, who had lived in Arizona and now resided in Texas with her family, had fallen ill back in October with lung cancer. It had spread faster than anyone of us had feared, always thinking there was a treatment option out there that would be the magical cure, but there wasn't. My heart dropped as he relayed the events that had occurred since the New Year and the looming prognosis. The cancer had indeed spread rapidly, and my aunt, my mother's sister, whom I always looked up to and adored like a daughter was supposed to look up to her own mother was given a death sentence. Doctors said she had weeks left, that there was nothing more they could do for her. The family was devastated and was advised to make her the most comfortable as possible as she got her final wishes in order.

My heart fell out of my chest onto the floor. I was in shock. I called home right away knowing full well that I would be making an emergency flight back to Texas where she lived with her husband and two young girls.

How could life offer such a double-edged sword? In one night, I met the most amazing man only to find out I would be losing one of the most influential women in my life. My stomach was upset, it felt like a violent tornado had swept through and left a cavity of mangled emotions, and I was unable to calculate the level of devastation.

I would need this new-found confidence I had acquired for more than just socializing. I would have to be composed and ready for whatever lay ahead. I looked up to both my aunt and uncle and knew they possessed immense strength as individuals and as a couple. They were an army family who had faced multiple tours to the Middle East, years at a time apart, but nothing could compare to the battle at hand. In 48 hours, I would be back in the United States, and I would be confronted with an experience I never saw coming.

Thinking back to that night, the events all seemed to mesh together, going from one place to another, dancing, giggling and radiating beauty and peace. Time just stood still, and before I knew it, it was morning. I had felt like I was on top of the world. Nothing really had changed but my perspective, and that was all that was needed to draw reciprocating energy. That may sound really spiritual, and I guess it was. When I changed my outlook on my life, when I decided to commit my own energy to myself and my ambitions, I just naturally started to draw attention. It had been the same way with Stephen when we met. I wasn't looking, content with myself and where I was going in life. I was focused inward on my own happiness, and that is when, like a lightning bug in the night, happiness out of nowhere found me.

Okay, I have to admit, I talked to a lot of people that night. Quite a few friends that I wasn't expecting to run into were there, and I spent the majority of my time catching up on what was new in their lives from their travels to promotions and sharing my new exploits, or at least my intentions for the upcoming months. I had only submitted my application. It wasn't a sure thing, at least not yet.

When I received a friend request from the random gentleman I pulled aside from the crowd that night, I was a little surprised. How did he find me? Considering he discovered me online reassured me that I still had some inhibitions; even with a couple of glasses acting against me, I hadn't given a complete stranger my phone number.

I remembered our conversation, and now I could put a name to his face. Before the club was packed, the music blaring, and even in the close proximity, I found it hard to follow word for word our conversation.

Bartosz was his name, and he took no time messing around. He was straightforward and to the point. He asked if we could meet for brunch on Sunday, and I kindly accepted the invitation even though I knew I would be leaving for the States over the next two weeks. What would it hurt? Thinking the whole while, what are you doing, another stranger? I guess old patterns are hard to break. I fall for strangers, no, not exactly, that sounds desperate and perverted, but rather I give chances. What could I say, I was enticed by a man I had only spoken to for five minutes in the club before hurrying off into the night like Cinderella. I hadn't left a glass slipper per se, having told him only my name, he made quick work on social media. He had made an impression, and I would rather meet him before I left rather than let the night fade into a distant memory.

Stepping off the tram, I was rushing from the gym back to my apartment. I was running late, and the rain was not helping. Dodging puddles, I definitely wore the wrong shoes for this occasion! Reaching for my cell phone tucked away in the depths of my purse, through a reservoir of odds and ends, I received a message to look for the blue car parked curbside out in front of my apartment building where Bartosz waited. Anxious, I opened the door to be greeted by a handsome man sitting in the driver's seat.

Was this the right car? A scarf tied around his neck dressed immaculately as the night we met, he was the same man from before, refined and gorgeous. Why should I be surprised, that was the way Europeans dressed, especially in Brussels. They were always keeping up with appearances much like the French. I felt a little out of place after having blown off some steam at the gym for the past 90 minutes trying to get my mind off my family matters back in Texas. I had only freshened up quickly before putting on my high heeled rubber rain boots and running out the door to catch the tram.

Not having any expectations for our date was a good thing. Before I always had some sort of picture in mind of how things would play out or what type of guy sat across from me. This time I was in the dark. We had spoken briefly and what I remembered did not give the slightest clue as to the type of individual who sat gazing into my eyes. With the rain coming down we pulled out onto the street to find a café that was actually open on a Sunday. A simple task you would think, but most restaurants and shops do not do business on Sundays, thought to be a day of rest. Absurd to most Americans, it is quite a normal practice in Europe. We finally found a little corner café, a cozy little spot, with a sleek interior and welcoming staff. It was Greek if I remember right. Many of the tables were messy, dirty plates and silverware, signifying they had been busy, but as the lunch hour slipped into late afternoon, the patrons had long departed leaving us a very intimate setting, very much unlike our first meeting.

I sat back in my chair to watch it unfold as if I were sitting in a cinema watching, eyes on the silver screen. Rather than directing the conversation, which I had the tendency to do, almost like an interview, I sat idle, waiting for him to make the first move. This time would be different. I was different.

We talked about our lives, where we were from, why we were in Belgium, and what we did for a living. All the typical questions, the usual first date candor. It wasn't awkward or forced like so many times before. It was a natural conversation of curiosity and fascination. A pleasant change from many dates I had pursued in Brussels, where the men were egotistical and smug. We talked about our travels, where we had been, and where we could see ourselves living one day. I felt a little tongue-tied as we both worked out our futures. We had made these plans as individuals, but somehow, we were contemplating if the same plans would account for two. I had never mentioned it before, but it was a peculiar moment for me. After being on my own for a little over two years, I had gotten very comfortable just being "me." I had become very independent, even borderline selfish. I didn't have to worry or account for a plus one in my life's equation, but maybe I would have to start factoring it in. I am not going to deny it. All the while, we were having a conversation I was playing out if the man that sat across the table from me was "the one." When weighing the pros and cons, I could actually see myself consenting to adding a partner to my dream.

Maintaining the outward appearance that I was not drawn to him, I just sat back in my chair sipping white wine from Greece, perplexed. I had not felt this way in so long. I didn't want to revert to old behaviors and patterns, wishful thinking, creating a vision that wasn't in line with reality. I was reserved. He was exactly what I wanted in a man. It was as if someone had tapped into my psyche where I had created an image or a list of the things that were make-or-break in my ideal depiction of a healthy relationship, and the blueprint of the man that sat there before me was drawn up in the exact proportions.

When dessert was offered, we ordered two, baked feta cheese with honey and nuts and homemade baklava. I have an awful sweet tooth, and he indulged it. What was I getting into? He was perfect!

Chivalry was not dead. I felt like a queen as he escorted me to the car. He held out his arm for me to hold tight to and made sure I was under the umbrella as the raindrops fell on his head. He was creating quite an impression.

Later on that day, after he had dropped me back to my apartment, I returned to reality. He asked me when he could see me again, and I had to confront the honest truth that I had to leave the following morning for two weeks to visit my family in Texas. I didn't go into great detail, I just left it that my aunt had fallen ill and I needed to be by her side.

Without hesitation, Bartosz offered to take me to the airport. I would have been content to take the train, but alright, sure, if the offer was up for the taking, I would indulge him.

WISDOM 1 SELF-LOVE IS A PRACTICE

Self-love is a concept that is all the rage today, people saying you "have to love yourself more...invest in yourself," but so often times, we are confused to actually what is meant by having compassion for yourself. We are so comfortable with loving and supporting others- listening to them, helping them and appreciating them- but when it comes to ourselves, love is often just a feeling that finds itself at the bottom of our to-do list and not something we prioritize or practice daily.

Since my parents' divorce, I came to realize I was always looking for outside validation. Maybe it was the product of toxic parenting, two adults more consumed by their own circumstances than their obligation to actually parent, but I never felt like I was enough. I judged and questioned my worth and never owned the confidence I asserted. I tried so hard to seek their approval, to go above and beyond in school, at work, in life, but to what end? I was lost, seeking love in all the wrong places. I had no model to teach me otherwise.

As a yoga teacher, I could go on and on about filling your cup full before helping others, but I was deaf to my own instruction. It wasn't until I made the choice to chart my own destiny, first by moving abroad and second by following my own life's calling and not giving into someone else's business pursuits, did I finally understand what all those gurus before me were really talking about. When I finally took the risk, applying for my independent status to stay in Belgium, did I actually feel an overwhelming sense of assurance that this was what genuine self-love was all about.

For some self-love may sound egotistical or narcissistic, but it is far from it. To be in a healthy relationship with someone else, we must first take care of ourselves. I know that society has shaped most of us to believe that putting ourselves first or being "selfish" is wrong, but if we were truly acting selfish, then we would be actively getting ahead in life at the expense of another. And that is not what self-love is at all.

Self-love should be at the root of all we do, but the rush of modern life so often gets in the way. Because of this pressure, most of our time each day engaging in activities that sustain us, rejuvenate us and help us evolve is often sacrificed. It is important we remember that there is so much more to life than achieving success, making money and even caring for others.

Many of us think we have an adequate amount of self-love in our lives as we take care of our basic needs, like having a roof over our heads, a job that pays the bills and a vacation occasionally, but it goes much deeper than that. Self-love is putting yourself first and foremost, nurturing love and respect for who you are as an individual no matter the situation or the company you are with.

Taking an honest feat of self-exploration, looking at the inner workings and driving force behind your life is a necessity, not a luxury. It is not a one-time act but should be a consistent part of our lives. We need this base of understanding of our own wants, needs, fears and desires in order to be able to live fully.

Incongruent living is exhausting. So often we find ourselves compromising in life, working at jobs that are less than satisfying, ignoring our own health and well-being at the expense of taking care of others. Cultivating self-love drives our ability to be fully and completely knowing of ourselves. When we have this understanding and acceptance of ourselves, which is so much more than just a feeling, it can be seen in the mirror and felt by those around you.

I experienced the magic firsthand. I felt my confidence rise, and I was steadfast in my resolve. I chose to take a more taxing path, one that would be laden with challenges and expense, but it was mine to take. That made all the difference. I had never set out on an adventure of such magnitude, but in doing so, I felt free to pursue that which made me feel alive and whole. It was electrifying, and this magnificent energy was a magnet for those around me, so much that the man of my dreams was drawn to me from the crowd.

Fostering richer, fuller relationships with others takes a commitment, and that commitment is the one you have with yourself. Love starts with you!

The time you devote to enriching your spirit will invigorate you and help cultivate a more peaceful way of being and more joy in your life.

CHAPTER 12

AN UNEXPECTED GOODBYE

**"Goodbyes are not forever. Goodbyes are not the end.
They simply mean I'll miss you until we meet again."
-Unknown**

Greeting me with a friendly smile, the shuttle driver helped me with my luggage before we embarked making small talk about where I had just flown in from over the short jaunt from the arrivals terminal to the rental car pickup area. Considering it was such a late hour, I was surprised how social everyone seemed. Even the rental car agent, who assumed I would be the last customer for the night, was courteous as he ushered me out with a set of keys to my car parked under a dimly lit street lamp tucked close to the barbed wire fence that lurked under the US Highway 281 overpass.

Sliding into the driver's seat, it dawned on me I hadn't driven a car in over nine months. I had become so adept to downtown living, relying primarily on public transport to get around, that I didn't know if I remembered how to operate this vehicle, but just like riding a bike, one never forgets. Putting the key in the ignition, I started the engine, and it all came flooding back to me.

It felt foreign to me to be surrounded by the English language everywhere I went. Yes, all of my friends back in

Belgium had spoken English to me, but it was the background noise that I found pacifying. It hadn't dawned on me until now how I just tended to drown out this chatter as white noise if it was in a foreign tongue, which actually gave me a lot of space to be in my thoughts. Standing in the line at the gas station, where I picked up a quick cup of watered-down coffee, I could not only hear and pay attention to the clerk taking my payment but the customer in line behind me having a conversation with his girlfriend. I found myself distracted by two men talking about the weather as they made a quick beeline to the Red Box to rent a movie. I felt inundated by so much extra information I wasn't able to retain it all, nor did I need to. I knew reverse culture shock existed, but this was the first time I was experiencing it. I hadn't lived abroad for that long, but I felt like a visitor in my own country.

The porch light was on as I pulled into the drive. Parking the car, I took a breath to compose myself before grabbing my suitcase from the trunk and heading to the front door. As I stepped onto the porch, my uncle emerged with tired eyes giving me a warm hug whispering a quiet welcome. It was late, and the family was fast asleep, having called it a night long ago. I could tell that the devastating prognosis about my aunt's limited chance of survival was taking its toll on my uncle as he helped me up the stairs to my cousin's bedroom, my makeshift guest room for the next two weeks.

The warm presence of family was a welcoming sensation in the face of dreadful despair.

Having recently retired from the army, my uncle put his over twenty years of medical training to use nursing his dying wife. He was juggling his role as a father and husband with being the primary caretaker. Traveling from Georgia, his parents were also there offering help in every way possible, but my uncle carried the brunt of the burden. He was the cornerstone, the rock that everyone would use to lean on. He put forth a strong facade, just like a soldier on the front lines, but I could tell he was aching inside. Caught up in his duty as a nurse, he hardly slept, lying awake at night worried, listening, and waiting. Distracted, he didn't have time to cope with the feelings of fear and untimely loss that he was inevitably facing.

My aunt was a fighter. Her spirit alone gave hope that she would pull through. Every morning I would get up long before dawn adjusting to the time zone change. Rather than tossing and turning, I would creep down the softly lit staircase to the kitchen, trying not to wake anyone along the way. The coffee pot was set on a timer, and not long after I tip-toed through the darkness to the dining table, my aunt would appear. The cancer had filled her lungs with fluids, and she had trouble breathing. The drugs the doctors prescribed only provided mild relief from the arduous pain. Her nights were short, making long mornings. She would try to stomach breakfast, but even that had become difficult. Her body had started to sink in, her cheeks were sagging, and her skeletal frame was all too apparent through the loose-fitting clothes she wore. My once healthy and voluptuous aunt looked like she had been starved. This was not the case of course, but the drugs and cancer in combination made nourishment nearly impossible. She had lost so much weight that when I went to help her change her clothes, I felt like I had to handle her with care, like a delicate piece of porcelain, that if I held too tight, I might bruise or break her causing unnecessary pain.

Resilient, she never ceased to amaze me. She was still working from home finding time to send out emails and organize her days' agenda between doctors' appointments and family visits. I would sit at the table, warming my hands around a steaming mug of coffee with my own computer in front of me. We made time to talk candidly about her fears as tears welled in her eyes and what she would miss most when she was gone. Somewhere deep down, I believe she knew her time on earth was near.

The day before I left Brussels my aunt had called me. I had already bought my plane tickets and was packing my things when she told me not to come. I don't know if she felt like it was an awful expense having to come all that way or self-sacrificing, but I would never have given up those precious moments for want of money. She didn't have to be altruistic; nothing in this world, not even her own request would have stopped me from being there.

We had a close relationship. I remember growing up in rural Iowa, sleeping over at my aunt's house every other weekend. We would order pizza, watch reruns of old soap operas and paint our nails. She felt like the big sister I never had. Nothing really changed when she moved to Texas in her late twenties, what was once a one night every other week was a short plane ride and a week vacation in what then seemed like another planet. Texas had seemed at the time to be worlds away to my younger, untraveled self. If only that little girl from Iowa could see me now. Would she believe me if I told her the places she would see and the people she would come to meet, that all her dreams would eventually come true?

My aunt and uncle had waited to get married. They were in their thirties when they said their vows. They were wiser and knew what they wanted. They shared stories from their starry-eyed romance, long highways, and travels through the night to be in each other's arms.

I still remember one conversation in particular where I was sitting in my car parked in my ex-boyfriend's driveway. I had been in the process of moving out of Joshua's house, and I was having a hard time coming to terms with all the lies I had allowed myself to be fooled by, the five years I felt I wasted on a man who didn't invest the same amount of love into our relationship as I had. My aunt could relate as she helped me through the hardships I faced in the relationship.

My aunt's voice still remains clear in my mind. Sitting in that driveway all alone in my car, crying, holding tight to the cell phone in my hand. Even after all these years have passed I still remember her saying on the other end of the line, "Emmy, you will know when you find the one. There is no way to describe it, but somewhere deep down, you will feel it. The man that walks into your life will help you understand why all the others never clicked. He will make you smile like you never have before. He will support you and be all you ever wanted. You won't have to make concessions or excuses because he will be enough."

I told my aunt about Bartosz, this man I just met only days before unexpectedly in a night club in Brussels. I explained we had only gone out on one date before he offered to collect me for the airport, and thank the Lord he did. I told my aunt how I was quickly working to make arrangements to come back to the United States, that I had to get my classes covered and inventory planned for the time I would be away. The night before I left, I was packing until 3 am, and if it was not for Bartosz ringing my doorbell at 7 am, I would never have made my flight. Still lying warm under the covers, I woke in a frenzy, throwing my dress over my head and sliding on my leather boots, I grabbed my luggage and raced down the stairs. Clearly disheveled I opened the front door, and there he was. He was quite a gentleman never making mention that morning that it was a close call, that he dodged in and out of traffic to make sure I made it to the departures terminal before the check-in closed. I wonder what he thought he was getting himself into.

My aunt could see I was somewhat preoccupied, and she thought it was cute. She was happy for me. Bartosz and I had been in contact exchanging messages since I had arrived, and she could tell I was infatuated by this mystery man. Confessing Bartosz had made an impression on me, I was getting a bit ahead of myself reconfiguring my future to account for his presence in it.

I had mentioned to him that I had plans to go to Amsterdam when I returned. It had been a trip I had been arranging for some time, but when I had to drop this unexpected voyage to the States into my budget, I didn't think I would end up going. Without hesitation he interjected, he thought it was a wonderful idea in fact, and if I were still up to it and could get the time off, he would design a weekend get-away to the Netherlands upon my return.

My aunt, who knew me almost better than I knew myself said, "Emmy, it sounds like you found your match, just by the way you speak of him." She would never meet him in person, this man of mystery, but she advised me, "Don't get so caught up living your life that you forget to make time for him."

Hearing her voice and seeing her in the last few weeks of her precious life was worth every penny that it cost me to be there. She reminded me of the value of life. It wasn't enough just to exist, but how important it was to be the star of your own show. She had so many stories to share, life experiences she had accumulated that made her special. Just simply sitting over coffee with her in the morning listening to her recall her trip to San Francisco to visit Alcatraz and how she and her daughters flew to see their father when he was stationed in Seoul, South Korea. She too was the product of a small town and had stepped out into the world full of adventure.

She was very special to me, as she was to our entire family. My mother flew in from Phoenix to be by her sister's side. I can't say that they had a great relationship, but my mother had wanted to make amends with her little sister. Regarding my mother and I, we kept our distance. Our relationship still had never been fully repaired. There was a distance that was very present, a cold brick wall that stood between us, and we couldn't seem to dismantle our differences. I tried to go there with an open mind, that if my mother would act compassionately toward the family and even myself, I would try to make amends, but I could see through her, she was insincere. On the nights where the family would stay up watching movies and eating popcorn, my mother would get gussied up in her short mini skirt and revealing neckline to go out for the night to some rodeo bar with heaven knows what character from her rolodex of men. I know she cared for her sister very much, but I didn't feel that flaunting oneself at a bar was appropriate for the situation.

When the time came for my mother to depart, she hugged my frail aunt. She proceeded to say her goodbyes to the rest of the family, embracing my cousins, my uncle and his parents, but when it came to me, she didn't even make an effort to meet my eye. I just stood in the kitchen astounded by her insolence. I was her child, and she was the parent, not the other way around. As if I were nothing to her, she turned and walked out the door with her suitcase in hand.

Being back in the United States for this occasion was nothing short of emotionally exhausting. I was in a position where my family needed me the most. Never would I have thought I would be accompanying my aunt to doctors appointments. She was in her late forties, far too young I thought, but cancer has no prejudice. I accompanied my aunt and uncle to church where we spoke openly to the priest about arranging my aunt's last wishes. We discussed her will and when it would be appropriate to bring their daughters, my cousins, up to speed about their mother's health condition. Everyone had their opinions. Some still believed there was hope. I believed in miracles too, but the facts were quite clear. My aunt's health was deteriorating rapidly, and the doctors were unable to offer any recourse.

I never really cried or showed weakness even in the days after I returned to Belgium. Maybe I was in shock, this had hit our family like a freight train, full thrust with no signs of stopping until I received the phone call. I had hugged my aunt for what would be the last time as I was walking out the door for the airport. I had stowed away a few pictures of her from an album that was lying on the coffee table. Memories of her I would keep in my possession. I can still remember her feeble embrace before I turned to walk away. When I heard the words on the other side of the line I felt my heart sink to the depths of my chest, yet no tears welled in my eyes.

What was wrong with me? I couldn't understand it. A woman I loved so deeply departed from my life, and I was without feeling, numb to the outside world. I had a hard time expressing my emotions, letting people in, and showing them my most vulnerable side.

For so long, I had been on my own in the world. I had to be strong and independent. I had to toughen up, hiding my more feminine side. I guess I had got used to it. For the first time in a long time, I had someone there by my side who was genuine, caring and offered the love I had longed for and that I could never find in my past relationships. He beckoned me to show my softer side. Bartosz had entered my life in a moment of great anguish and of change. I was losing someone very dear to my heart, but at the same time, I had gained another. I found myself opening up to the thought that I could actually fall in love with this man, and it could be real. The love my aunt had spoken to me about, the love she knew, the love I dreamed of, and only ever wished I would find had found me.

WISDOM I LIFE IS IMPERMANENT

Losing my aunt to cancer was a reminder that life is precious and that in moments, everything can change. When I found myself in a state of grief and denial, I found solace in the concept of mindfulness, a Buddhist teaching deeply connected to impermanence.

Mindfulness is a way of life in which we become aware of the present – our thoughts and feelings, our physical experience, and the world around us; it is much like reflection, but as an active practitioner you are not looking at the past but rather the very moment you are living. Fostering acceptance that there is no permanence or guarantee we can look at the present and examine what we are genuinely feeling.

How did embracing mindfulness help me in my time of grief? There are two common ways many of us cope with grief – we become completely consumed and feel trapped by anguish. Or, from fear of that, we try to circumvent the pain and emotions so we can *move on*.

Mindfulness reminds us that pain and sorrow are natural human emotions and are fleeting. Does this mean grief can be vanquished completely? Of course not. But it does mean that it will change shape and form; it will ebb and flow. Some days will be excruciating, and some days you will find yourself laughing for no particular reason. Mindfulness reminds us that our grief, like everything else, is impermanent and ever-changing. Once we accept this, even if only on a rational level, some of the need to avoid our grief starts to diminish. We can start noticing and accepting our grief for what it really is, a passing storm cloud that will soon pave the way for clearer blue skies.

CHAPTER 13

WHAT OUR FUTURE HOLDS

"In the end, we only regret the chances we didn't take, the relationships we were afraid to have, and the decisions we waited too long to make."
-Lewis Carroll

Crazy maybe, but I went along with the plan. Taking the initiative, Bartosz organized a weekend getaway in the Netherlands. I never had a man do all the planning. I guess most of the men figured I loved organizing the details, so they just left me to it, but it was incredibly nice to have the roles reverse for a change. Secretively, Bartosz made all the arrangements while I was still in the States and said nothing about them. When he picked me up at the airport in Brussels, he was still hesitant to divulge any details about our impending weekend adventures. Dodging my questions as if I were speaking in tongues, he said he wanted it to be a surprise. He also wanted to take me out on a second date to affirm his feelings were real towards me before gallivanting off to some romantic hideaway. We hadn't seen one another in over two weeks, but that was not to say we weren't entirely infatuated with each other. We had exchanged messages every day while I was away, morning, noon and well into the evening considering we were not in the same time zone. The entire time I was gone,

I was held captive in suspense as to what was to come when I returned. Was I embarking on a fairytale love affair one reads about in a book or witnesses on the big screen?

My friends thought I was a bit out of my mind when I told them I was driving to Amsterdam for a long weekend. Who was this mystery man they had never even met? Even my friends that were with me in the club that night had a hard time recalling who I was talking about. "What man, you were all over the place talking to men?" All they knew was what I told them, and in reality, I knew very little. To them, I was behaving like I was a naïve teenager running off with an older man to god knows where putting myself in danger and not thinking about the consequences of my actions.

Blatantly I pushed aside what some would call sensible advice. I didn't want to hear it. As I saw it, Bartosz was feeding into my adventurous spirit by taking the reins and planning a relaxing weekend away. His intentions were sincere, I could feel it. After spending two weeks back in the United States dealing with matters of loss and the untimely death of my aunt I needed some time to get out of my head, and he empathized with what I was going through as his uncle had recently passed. They too were very close.

I had explained to him that in the past, I never really missed my family or had this yearning that most people have living in a faraway land. I guess either coming from a family broken by divorce or having lived in another state for eight years, only making it back once or twice a year had made me hard, resilient to longing. Speaking over the phone once every month, never face to face on Skype was enough. My family had no need for such technology. If I went into too much detail about my life I felt like I was boasting or unrelatable, and I tried to keep that to a minimum.

It was not until I got the call that my aunt had passed away in her sleep that I felt this overwhelming nostalgia, a yearning for those I left behind. I felt like I needed to be there, but I wasn't. It would have been easy to have locked myself away in my apartment until the sadness wept from my eyes, but I couldn't seem to bring myself to tears. In the dark crevices of my mind, I kept replaying memories from my childhood, painting our nails, and having my aunt curl my hair for the Christmas pageant. I couldn't take it; I needed something, anything to break the cycle and the trip to Amsterdam, the "Venice of the North" was pinnacle to finding my way out of the shadows and back into the light.

Arriving under the yellow glow of street lamps, we pulled into a small, dank parking lot on the outer edge of the city. Collecting our belongings from the trunk, the tram was footsteps from where we left Bartosz's Beamer in a crowded lot protected by a metal barbed wire security fence. We were staying on a lavish houseboat docked on one of the canals near the center of the city, but I didn't know this yet. It was all still a surprise. I hadn't been able to break him, not even when we met for wine and cheese at a small wine bar called Oeno TK very close to mine for our second date. Not explaining, he just said it made more sense to park the car on the outskirts rather than hassle with finding something closer.

We arrived starving. Having left Brussels after work, we began to realize we totally overlooked dinner. Hitting the freeway, we were in the fast lane to get out of town.

Even though it was only a little over a three-and-a-half-hour drive to Amsterdam, we were famished by the time we arrived at the houseboat Bartosz had rented. Well, it was part of the houseboat; the owners lived in the residence below deck, and as architects, they had designed the upper floor to be a chic, modern apartment with a minimalist maritime theme welcoming guests from near and far.

A little after eleven in the evening our host was sad to break the news to us that even restaurant takeaway would be hard to come by at such a late hour, but in consolation, she offered what she could. Carrying up a pot of warm pasta with a roasted garden vegetable marinara from their kitchen nestled in their cozy quarters below deck, she arrived more than happy to dish up two plates for us.

Not wanting to make a fuss, but quite hungry, we accepted our hosts' generosity. A little past midnight, we sat down to the most delectable meal of homemade fettuccine tossed in a marinara with roasted carrots, mushrooms, eggplant and zucchini. By candlelight we settled into our luxurious second story deck top apartment. Taking in the magnificent views of centuries-old townhomes, I wanted to pinch myself. Was this all a dream?

Bartosz had done his homework, maybe too well. He impressed me. I had never been treated so well before, where I felt like the red carpet had been rolled out under my feet. I was surely hallucinating. This couldn't be my life. Maybe this was how the other half lived. I wasn't sure. It was a whole new ballgame. This new-found lifestyle was a little overwhelming, intimidating, in fact. I was a small-town girl; I enjoyed the finer things in life once in a while, but not like this. For me, it seemed Bartosz lived his life this way. He drove a nice car, paid for everything, and held the door for me. He even found it somewhat offensive if I tried to reach for the handle. Maybe I had been treated horribly in the past, and this was what a true man should do for the woman he loves, chivalry, right, but it was all a bit alien to me.

Everything was new; this wasn't like any relationship I had in the past. There was no reference point to even compare. Deep down, I was scared. I feared that getting back into a serious relationship would destroy everything I had worked on over the last two years. I had rebuilt myself from the rubble. I had become a strong, independent woman. My ambitions, my dreams, would I have to give this all up for a man? Would I fall back into my old ways?

The beauty about Bartosz was that he was infatuated with me, the whole me, not wanting anything to change. Over the weekend, we had the opportunity to get to know one another even better, like peeling away the layers of an artichoke, discarding the tougher outer leaves to uncover the heart.

I'd had a couple of flings, short relationships since Joshua, but nothing stuck. The affairs had all been casual, never making a deep connection or a sound base for the future. There wasn't that spark that instilled a desire to invest more. I guess I was playing hard to get. It wasn't for lack of trying; I put myself out there, but it wasn't until I met Bartosz that I was presented with the entire package. This was the first time where everything seemed to fall into place. I was not only treated well, but I got this mental stimulation I was forever looking for but could never find. He worked in politics and was highly educated. We could hold a conversation about the impending European elections or the state of Cuban tourism. From discussing the Polish presence in the Battle of Britain to the last

German offensive at the Battle of the Bulge, we were interested in many of the same subjects.

I was thrilled to have so much in common. I wanted to see the places he had seen from Peru to Israel, Jordan to Greece. Bartosz, almost ten years my senior, with almost a decade experience in European politics, had traveled to many destinations in the world that I had not yet discovered. I lived vicariously through his stories, knowing one day we might get there together.

I had never felt such a connection to a man. We talked about what hadn't worked in our past relationships, the want to settle down or the inability to do so, what we wanted out of life, our careers, our families, and about our travels in the United States, where we had been and places we still wanted to see. As with the start of any great relationship, we were getting to know one another. Cuddling under a wool blanket with my head in his lap, I closed my eyes beneath the star-studded sky.

The next day we explored. Nervous, the butterflies in my belly would not restrain themselves. I couldn't believe we were walking hand in hand down cobblestone streets, along the canals. Partaking in the local culture, hopping in and out of coffee shops, the apprehension I had when I woke had vaporized by noon. Although smoking marijuana was not a regular pastime of mine, it was definitely an ice breaker. Laughing the entire afternoon, we realized we had gotten lost along the way. Backtracking and indulging our increasing appetites with local fare, we threw in the white flag and hailed a taxi to take us back to our hideaway, our pleasure trove for the night.

Snug under the covers wrapped in each other's arms, we relished the moment as the morning dawned. The grey sky peering through the windows offered a cozy backdrop for being lazy and staying in this enchanted wonderland. There was no sense of urgency to be anywhere. Work could wait.

The weekend was nothing short of magical, and it only left me wanting more. More of his time, exercising at the gym, shopping in the market, and meeting for coffee. Within weeks of dating, it felt like we had been together for a year. Valentine's Day was the week after we had returned from Amsterdam, and I couldn't have envisioned a better day. Without planning, we both went to work. Bartosz dropped me off at the spa after having stayed the night, and he headed off to work in the EU quarter. As the workday wound down, I found him parked out in front of the yoga studio after teaching my last class of the night, and as I opened the door, he presented me a dozen red roses. We both had our fitness apparel on and discussed going to the gym where we spent a couple of hours. At 10 pm, we arrived at my favorite sushi spot and celebrated our first Saint Valentine's together. I don't know how it could have gotten any better!

The relationship seemed to be moving at an accelerated pace until we hit a speed bump. Two months into our love story we hit a crossroads. A moment when politics impressed its importance onto our relationship.

I had one of two choices as I saw it. Bartosz would be away for almost three months in Poland running a political campaign for his boss. We had not even been together the same amount of time he anticipated he would be gone. It wasn't so much a discussion but a statement of fact. I didn't know what to say. He would be living in a hotel room in a small town southeast of Warsaw, and I would remain in Belgium. He would have to put in 15-16 hours a day working with little to no downtime to think of anything else.

There was nothing to discuss. I realized somewhere along the way we had arrived at a committed relationship. There was no threshold designating when we went from casual to serious, but we both acknowledged we were in it for keeps. If this was something he had to do, love would prevail. He wasn't offered a choice, nor was I. I had waited my whole life for my prince to appear and three months would come and go in comparison to a lifetime. There was no room for me on this campaign, nor would I want to put my life on hold.

'There is strength to withstand that which you think is unbearable.' Many nights I felt a longing for his strong body next to mine, but as I would slowly fall to sleep the morning would again wake. Every day would start anew and before we realized it the time was starting to pass us by. Over Easter Bartosz was able to take some time off from the campaign, just enough hiatus to slip away to Croatia for some much-needed rest and relaxation.

Flying into the regional airport in Zadar, it had been nearly a month since I saw his face. Yes, you would think Skype, but he was either dining with his boss at midnight setting the agenda for the next day or up at the break of dawn collecting volunteers to hand out flyers. He was on the road in a Mercedes van wrapped in their campaign slogan. I knew he was busy.

We spoke almost every day, but I wanted more. I desired his passionate embrace, the sweet taste of his lips on mine, and the way his smile would caress my heart from across the room. I waited in a little outdoor café overlooking the parking lot after landing in what I would term as my little piece of paradise, Croatia. The airport was nearly deserted. Early April, tourism was still slow, but soon enough crowds of holiday goers would infiltrate the coastal nation mid to late May as the temperatures would rise and the sea would become alight with sails.

Maybe I arrived early, or he was delayed. I had over an hour to myself sitting on the wooden terrace taking in the softness of the air perfumed by pine. I was alone, conscious of my mind and its wanderings. When things are going well, it never dawned on me to be self-reflective in contrast to times of trouble. I guess that was just how it worked. I never felt obliged to put pen to paper unless I had an issue to resolve or worry to articulate. I never just wrote in my journal for the sake of writing; there was always a reason behind giving my words substance.

It wasn't that I was out of sorts or had any great concerns weighing me down, but I had time on my side. It was a great opportunity to consider the good things I had going for me. I had just recently left my job at the spa and was in a unique position trying to find my way again. Sitting with almost the entire café at my disposal, there wasn't a soul to disturb my thoughts from pouring onto the scraps of paper laid out in front of me. I could outline my goals and what I wanted to achieve, weighing the hurdles that might appear in my way that could, in effect, hinder me from staying on course. The stopwatch was ticking the seconds away. How long could I stay in Europe now that I was no longer employed? If I did not resolve this pending issue, I had no future at all to look forward to, at least not on this continent. It was a burden I had to deal with, a consequence of choice. No different from before, it was a challenge I was forced to face. If I wanted to stay, I had to work for it, plain and simple. There were no handouts or tricks I could play.

I had become my own artist. I was creating a life where I felt both balance and engaged. I didn't need to have two jobs to make ends meet. Not everything relied so heavily on money, but more about the experience, and that was what I had found so attractive about the relationship Bartosz and I had. Yes, okay, I may be a little contradicting here, because I was very fortunate to find a man that had everything going for him. He had life experience, a stable job and was driven. Did this make things easier? Maybe. That is hard to say for certain. I believed we were on the same page, and that was what mattered most. No matter where we would go in life, we had the same philosophy that would pave the way to our version of happy-ever-after.

An hour quickly passed by as I scribbled my thoughts down on the scrap pieces of paper I slipped in my purse as I saw Bartosz's car turn into the desolate parking lot. The seconds seemed to slow in anticipation of his arrival. Driving 14 hours non-stop through the night he emerged from the driver's seat weary from the road. I welcomed him into my arms, wanting to hold him tight and never let him go.

Three months sure enough passed by, and before I knew it, he was back in my arms for good. He was tired and beat up from the campaign in Poland. The stress had taken its toll on his body. His hair was starting to gray, and his neck was marred by blemishes that were the effects of a demanding schedule. With little sleep and hardly a healthy diet, he looked broken. He was burnt out, and I could see it in his eyes. With over nine years of experience in politics, the fast-paced, political rat race was killing him, and it was all too apparent change would be needed if we were to live a happy, healthy life together.

Our relationship overcame this period apart, and it was time to start planning our future together. We had only been dating for five months, but we were making quick business of setting the wheel in motion. Questions fluttered through our minds like hummingbirds to a flower. There wasn't just one thought or idea to explore but a whole multitude of possibilities to contemplate. I had only lived in Belgium for a little over a year when we met, and I wasn't quite sure if I was ready to entertain leaving a place I felt so at home. Bartosz, on the other hand, had his fill of the city. In over nine years he had seen the city in its most favorable light and at its ugliest. Brussels, I would have to say looking back, could be defined by many conflicting words, wealth and poverty, culture and discrimination, success and struggle. I had for so long focused on the beauty and the good in the city that I overlooked the dark, ugly underbelly that Bartosz had grown to hate.

He had seen evil first hand when he was confronted by an Arab man beating a young woman at the City Center 2 Mall in downtown Brussels. As witness to this violence he did what I would want to think any respectable man would do and he pushed the assailant away from the victim only to hear the man angrily yell, "ma femme, ma femme," "my wife, my wife." It was a though he was saying his wife was his property, and it was his given right to strike her in public. Bartosz started to beat the man hoping the woman would run away, which she did, not telling what she would expect as punishment when and if she went home. Security rushed in, but to Bartosz's astonishment, he was the one they ascertained and held confined. The mall security who were of Middle Eastern descent had seen the attack, yet did nothing to help the innocent woman, but when the roles were reversed, and one of their own caught a fist in the face, they stepped in escorting Bartosz to his car and releasing the aggressor without charge.

When I boiled down my feelings and intuition, it dawned on me why was I putting up barriers to possibilities when my primary motivation moving abroad was to see, experience and enjoy all the marvels the world could offer. Brussels and Belgium for that matter was only a fragment of the whole, only a stepping stone to the next big thing, the next place I would call home.

Living in Belgium had given me a base, very much like my hometown in the United States. It would always be there for me to come back to if I ever lost my way.

Exploring our options, we narrowed our selection down to two. Poland versus Spain. Two very different countries. Europe, a complex map of nations, is by no means bigger than the United States. Some could compare crossing national borders to crossing state lines, but it is not quite that easy. Yes, with the European Union things have changed. For member countries, citizens can transverse borders more freely, living, working and studying abroad. Tourists no longer need visas or to exchange currencies, but each country differs significantly regarding customs, weather, politics, landscape, and most importantly, language.

Setting these two options on a scale was a tough decision. I recalled my own experience in Poland when I met Łukasz. I had found the country and its people very welcoming. One of the most attractive aspects for me, in particular, was the fascinating history the country possessed. Turbulent, yes, but not by choice. Its geographical position made it a target of conflict not only in World War II but also in the post-war era of Soviet occupation. Poland's history was plagued by conquest for centuries. Even in college, my undergraduate studies in history only scraped the surface of what there was to learn.

It wasn't that we had to make the decision overnight. Bartosz still had to finish out his contract which would take us to the end of the year, and we were only halfway through. I still had important tasks to tackle between now and then. My professional card application was still in process, and I wasn't guaranteed I would be approved even with the missing link in hand.

If I were rejected, our plans would be wasted. There was no reason for getting too ahead of ourselves. I wanted to make the right decision, and more importantly, I needed to see this application through before starting down another path. If I couldn't make it on my own in Brussels, how would I stand a chance in Poland or Spain? So many friends of mine had joked about getting married for papers, but that was out of the question. Maybe it was my pride or my ego, but I needed to prove to myself that it was within me to do this on my own. I didn't want to force our relationship to the next level. It would be too much, too soon. If we went down that road, I would never be able to live with myself. I could never take that kind of handout even from the man I loved. Moving forward did not involve taking the easy way out.

WISDOM | TAKE ACTION, DON'T WAIT

What will you learn if you take the road that is wrought in wear? We can come up with millions of excuses, yet none of them will be satisfying. To take the high road paved with challenges takes a dedicated effort. It is so easy to slip into that which is familiar, comfortable and frankly numbing, instead of recognizing that testing our will offers a bigger reward. Yes, we can justify the path of least resistance, but what will we gain from that concession?

There is a popular misconception often associated with new age spirituality that we are capable of wishing our dreams into reality. Maybe on some other level of consciousness, this is plausible, but here on earth, we actually need to act to see results. Vision is a wonderful companion to determination, but it can't accomplish anything on its own. When we concentrate on what we want and ask for it, we are initiating a conversation with the universe. Our desires, clearly defined, bring about a profound awareness and direct our attention towards opportunities that will help execute that ambition.

Many of us are scared to make that first step. Honestly, I was terrified. I was afraid of failing, but I convinced myself that if failing was the worst that could happen, at least it would be worth the try. I was okay with the repercussions. My self-esteem would be battered, but that would heal. What I wasn't comfortable with was living out the rest of my days wondering what if.

Hanging back, dreaming, waiting and watching others chase their ambitions may be right for a time, but this period of idleness must cease at some point if you are to ever start living. No one expects perfection, and failing gets a bad rap. We're human. Rather than waiting for the universe to hand us our dreams on a silver platter, it's best to ready ourselves for the fight.

One of the difficult facets about having a great vision is that when we actually execute it in real life, it often comes out looking entirely different than what we had hoped or, worse, it doesn't come out at all. But hey, that's okay. Moving abroad, I was convinced I would live in

Belgium for at least five, if not ten years, but that was all about to change or at least it was a possibility. The choice was mine to make.

Though your aspirations may evolve from your initial blueprint, it will still be your will that brought them to life.

CHAPTER 14

A BRUISED EGO

**"Failure is the opportunity to begin
again more intelligently."
-Henry Ford**

Rejection. When you think you have life in the palm of your hand, you have it all figured out and slowly like sand, it all slips through your fingers. A feeling that can be debilitating. It can wreak havoc on your self-esteem and image of self-worth.

Putting myself out on the live wire, I had applied for my independent status three months before my employment contract would end at the spa. The time approached quickly, and two weeks before I would turn in my keys and teach my last yoga class for this studio, I received a rejection letter from the Foreign Ministry. My application had been denied.

Written in French, I could piece together the main point which was plain as day. I had been rejected, wham, slap in the face, and knee to the gut! There I was moments before I walked through the door and retrieved my mail. I had a good day, no complaints, the weather was bad, but it was always bad, it was Brussels for goodness sake, rain was a constant. I go to open the letter expecting to celebrate only to find I want to hang myself on a damn clothesline, let my head sulk and die. Frustration escalating, I couldn't read French, well not all the legal jargon, you didn't meet such and such requirement, there is no demand in society and other nonsense lines. I needed help in deciphering what actually went wrong. I called up a dear friend, a colleague from the spa, Alberto. He was a young professional from Spain. I asked him to sit with me over coffee to explain what the authorities had given as reason for such action. He was gifted with the art of languages, speaking Spanish his native tongue, fluent English, he was nearly perfect at French and had some familiarity with Italian. Fortunately, he had time and was more than willing to help.

As we sat down early the next morning at Parlor Café, a locally owned eatery with eccentric charm, the smell of espresso from behind the counter drifting out into the crowded room, the staff was busy filling orders for those hustling in and out on the day's commute. Snuggling into two cozy armchairs near the rear of the café overlooking a beautiful terrace, we watched as the morning sun started to peek out from behind the storm clouds. The gray and the gloom, so typical of Brussels, made the rays of sunlight all the more reassuring that there was a bright side to every story. I just needed to discover what needed to be done to move on from this setback.

I had the night to sleep on it since receiving the letter in the post box. I must confess; I was in shock and a state of complete confusion. I'd felt defeated and may have overreacted. I had another friend that had applied for her professional card about the same time that I had, and she was approved right away. What did I do wrong? There must have been a mistake, but there wasn't.

It was all quite clear as my young Spanish colleague and I went over the document line by line. I had made an enormous error that was detrimental in showing my contribution to Belgian society. When I filed my application, I had simply filled out the paperwork without submitting any subsequent material to add value to my case. I needed to convince the authorities I was an esteemed member of society. With this statement, I needed to prove I was making an income to support myself, paying taxes, and could also contribute to the country's social security system.

The major difference when I applied for my professional card and when my friend did was that she sought an outside consultant. She had created a business plan with contacts, letters of recommendation, stats and figures supporting her estimated income and her impact on the market and potential growth. She had laid everything out in a neat and organized document outside of the formal application that detailed perfectly her objectives. It wasn't that I was lazy, but I was uniformed. I had gone to the administration office for social services, and they had just processed my file as though it were a one-size-fits-all case. The clerk behind the desk who sat across from me showed me the documents to sign and asked a few questions. It was done in the course of thirty minutes. I paid the fee and left. I didn't receive any guidance or advice that supporting materials, such as a business plan and client lists, would add significant weight to the application. I merely filed my documents as I had done many times before in a cookie-cutter fashion. In the end, there was no reason I didn't stand out from the hundreds of other applicants, immigrants and EU nationals alike trying to get the golden ticket to stay.

Fortunately, being denied wasn't terminal. The last few sentences in the rejection document outlined that I had the opportunity to dispute the decision and in doing so I would have to appear in front of a tribunal where the standing members would finalize their decision once and for all. It was advised that I bring a lawyer, and in this case, since my French was lacking, (who am I kidding, it was not existent) I thought it a very wise idea to heed the advice.

Okay, so the bad news wasn't the end of the world. It wasn't what I had anticipated, but it did force me to do my homework and hunker down. I had to fine-tune my career goals, which were interchangeable with my business plan and spend some quality time with my computer and friends who had gone through similar processes. In this exchange of information, I was referred to a lawyer and would soon be ready.

Looking back, failing at the time felt dreadful, the end of the line where I faced having to put my tail between my legs and go crawling home in defeat, but it was actually the best thing that could have happened. Failing made me go back and restructure my foundation. Setting my ego aside, I worked through various scenarios, doing research, and getting strong references so that when the time came to appear before the Ministry of Foreign Affairs, I would be prepared to fight.

The day finally came. Bartosz, my lawyer and a Belgian friend accompanied me to my appointment where I had to present my case to the tribunal. I was nervous. Tired from wondering what if, I was ready. It had been almost six months since I had started this entire process. My employment at the spa had ended two months before, and I was just busying myself, traveling to Croatia, the north of Poland and to Poperinge in West Flanders near the

French border until the day finally came. My lawyer and I reviewed my case in the hallway before we were called into the conference room.

In front of me sat four gentlemen. A representative from Wallonia, the French-speaking region of Belgium, an individual from Flanders, the Flemish or Dutch-speaking region, a high-ranking director from the ministry and an immigration officer. There was one additional man seated to my far left who was the curator. He brought us into the room and made the formal introduction of the proceedings that would take place over the next hour.

I felt like I was sitting on a hot plate being interrogated with a light glaring into my eyes. I wasn't sure if I was giving the right answers or if I was just babbling. Convinced I was doing well, my lawyer translated my responses thoroughly filling in the gaps with legal terminology when he deemed fit. Hard to read, the men who sat across the table from me were stern, professional, and took their jobs very seriously. Sitting in the middle wearing traditional apparel, green velvet shorts, suspenders and the same forest green blazer to match the trousers, the Director of Foreign Affairs took some serious convincing. He was a hard man to crack. He countered every response I had with another even more demanding question. He had reviewed my file thoroughly and was going to make a point to clear up any doubt he had in his mind before he would stamp his approval. The others listened intently only to interject with their agreement.

If that wasn't stressful enough, I was aware of the fact that I could be in violation of my visa. Considering the time when I started the application, it was still valid. Now six months later, I was starting to press the limits. I wasn't ready to say my goodbyes. Over the past year and a half,

I had made a home for myself. I was in a serious relationship, and I didn't want my dream to fade away.

It came down to final remarks. I had the opportunity to offer any last words of support that would be considered in my case.

Thoughts whirled through my mind. What could I say to turn the table in my favor? From the very first day I stepped foot onto Belgian soil I was having to explain myself. Why did I want to live in Belgium so badly? Why on earth did I choose this country over my homeland the United States or any other country for that matter? What made Belgium so special?

My case was genuine and straight from the heart. I had never been welcomed into a place as warmly as I had been in Belgium, and I was a well-traveled woman, at least on the European continent. A mix of expats and locals, once strangers, were now close friends. The type of friends I could count on and reach out to even in the direst situations. I had never felt this way before. I had a family here, a group of fascinating individuals from various backgrounds. I had a place in this world. The doors of opportunities that opened were only beginning to unfold, and the potential would abound. I had appeared on House Hunters International on cable television in the United States. I had been interviewed for the newspaper Le Soir on a couple of occasions in association to Bookalokal, a global community where I was a host and chef creating unique dining experiences in my home. I also appeared in and worked with the Belgian Beer and Food Magazine as their marketing and events specialist. I was out on the high sea and wanted to continue to ride the wave.

To that end, the gentleman from Flanders stood up to thank me, he had never heard such praise for his country. When you are an outsider looking in, you see things differently. You have not grown jaded and weary from the same old everyday affairs. A fresh perspective can make all the difference in opening even the most tired eyes to those things that had become filler, background noise in a comfortable life.

I was excused. Leaving the conference room, I rejoined Bartosz and my friend in the waiting area where a man from South Africa awaited his turn to be grilled. We took a seat and not moments later, the curator appeared. Speaking in French with my lawyer, he turned to translate. I would be notified by phone in three hours of the tribunal's decision. I was free to leave.

With a sigh of relief, I stepped into the elevator. All I could do now was wait.

The phone rang; on the other end of the line, my lawyer announced the news. I was approved. My hard work paid off. What a relief. I had made it happen on my own. The rejection setback was only a minor inconvenience compared to the wealth of knowledge and experience I could now share with other expats facing similar situations. I no longer had to worry about the possibility of having to return to the United States prematurely. I was given 18 months to get my life sorted out and get down to business.

WISDOM | FAILURE

I tacked this experience on the board under Major Life Lessons 101. Up against the odds, I hit a pitfall that not only could have detoured my future in a direction I was not ready to take, but it was a stab to my ego. I was humbled. At one moment I had experienced an abundance of self-love and admiration for the life I had built, and the next, I stumbled to my knees. But this set back wasn't permanent, and failure wasn't the end of the road.

The word failure conjures up a very simplistic way of thinking that permits only two possibilities: failure or success. Few things in life are black and white, yet much of our language reads as if they are. When we consider something we have done, or ourselves, as a failure, we cloud the truth and muddle the issue at hand. Not to mention, we hurt ourselves. All you have to do is speak or read the word failure to experience the gravity it holds. When you put your mind to it, judging yourself, comparing actions to that of others only leads down a dark path of shadows and fear. We have all done it. Self-loathing is a hopeless funnel plunging us into the depths of negativity and despair.

Unfortunately, in our culture today, failure has come to represent the worst feasible outcome. Failure is a word so laden with such apprehensive and unconscious energy that we can all serve to benefit from consciously examining our use of it, because the speech we use with ourselves and others influences the way we think, feel and are perceived in society.

Acknowledging the problem is the first step towards finding the solution. Sounds like a self-help organization, right? Well, we can help ourselves through these inconvenient circumstances by being gentle and compassionate with ourselves and others.

Next time you feel like a failure, fear the possibility of failure or judging someone else, know that you are under the influence of an outdated way of perceiving the world.

When the word failure arises in conversation, it's a call for us to apply more tolerance to the matter at hand. When you become consciously aware of the word and the weight it holds, you will not fall victim to its darkness. In your own daily speech, you may choose to forgo using the word failure altogether. This might inspire you to express the truth of the situation more clearly and concisely, opening your mind to subtleties and possibilities the word failure would never have permitted.

CHAPTER 15

LIVING IN THE PRESENT

"I've found if you love life, life will love you right back."
-Arthur Rubinstein

Sitting on an outdoor garden patio paved with stone on a sultry summer evening, I introduced my husband to old friends who had just arrived in Barcelona from Phoenix. I couldn't believe nearly three years had passed since I had seen them last. Born in Serbia, Sergio and Lana have lived over the past twenty years, most of their adult lives, in the United States. They would be the first to affirm that they have an American perspective on life though their roots still have a place in European soil. They spend a couple of months a year, primarily in the summer during the school break in Beograd, the capital of Serbia, where they still own a downtown apartment. Spending time visiting family and friends they give their children a taste of Europe without having to commit fully. As parents, they immerse their children in the culture and language that they were born into. Two months abroad quickly pass, and they are back in the United States, back to the fast-paced life running the kids to and from school, operating their own restaurant, and arranging extra-curricular activities from soccer practice and volleyball games to church-related functions. I have seen Lana and Sergio's children grow, and they would agree that the kids have been "Americanized" in all senses of the word. They have become reliant upon the latest technology and having all the comforts and conveniences at their fingertips, lavish cars, a big house, a pool and all the space anyone could ever desire.

The first day we met I was uncomfortable, having changed so much since the last time I had seen them, I was full of nerves. Anxious about our meeting, I wondered what they would say about my grand adventure. I was now married, living the life I had always told them I wanted for myself. Lana, much like my aunt, had always believed I was born on the wrong continent. Sergio was not as whole-heartedly convinced though he knew I would have to find out for myself before I would rest. Far removed from the life I once lived, their visit was a friendly reminder of where I had come from. The beauty was I didn't have to dwell in the past. Their presence did not invoke a stroll down memory lane, but it allowed me a sneak peek into the life I could have been living if I had never taken the gamble I had.

In thinking about our upcoming meeting, I wondered if they too had changed. I often fear that I cannot relate to the friends I once had because we might no longer share commonalities that had once linked us together. This wasn't so much the case between Lana, Sergio and I because we had both experienced the best of both worlds, having lived in the US and Europe. Breaking through the discomfort and awkwardness within a few minutes of exchanging hellos and friendly small talk, we quickly fell back into the friendship I once cherished. I was thankful that we could fall back into the rhythm we once had before like no time had passed.

Lana is one of my best friends. She is one of those women I idolize for her strength. Diagnosed with stage four breast cancer at the young age of 42, she had faced death lying in a hospital bed after she had breast implants and a spinal fusion, frail and defenseless in the battle for her life. In and out of treatment centers, seeking out the most advanced research and diagnosis in a war that, in my eyes, is now becoming an epidemic. An emotional sigh of relief escaped my body when I received word that her doctor had treated the disease, and she was found to be the victor in the fight. She was cleared of any trace of cancer and put under quarterly observation.

After I turned thirteen, I never really had that mother figure to look to for advice and inspiration. Similar to the role my aunt had played in Texas, only a phone call away, Lana was that person I could meet with face to face for a coffee or a margarita at a Mexican cabana filling the void providing friendship and motherly insight. She was one of the very few I felt comfortable leaning on when times got tough. She knew both Joshua and me since the time we started our relationship. She saw us grow in our love together and watched it slowly over time wither away until its abrupt end. Joshua and I had both worked for their family-owned restaurant at one point in our careers, and it was their daughter's birthday party that Joshua never showed up to because he had spent the night at the casino.

Lana was straight forward, honest and true. She didn't put up a front or paint herself out to be anything pretentious. She was open-minded and saw the big picture asking questions of the norm rather than accepting the propaganda so many feed into. She always believed in me. She knew my heart belonged "out there somewhere," on the other side of the globe, in some foreign land yet to be discovered. I remember her saying once or twice that even though I may have been born an American, my spirit would thrive in Europe. For many reasons, Europe had always spoken to me, and she supported me when I answered its call.

Lana remarked when I returned from the five months I spent abroad after Joshua that I looked good. I had gained weight and looked healthy. But now, three years later, I had made a remarkable transformation from the girl they once knew into an admirable woman.

We moved to Barcelona, a city so much the opposite of Brussels that you could compare it to moving from Washington DC to San Diego. We went from the center of politics to a life by the sea.

When I moved to Brussels, I envisioned it being my home for the foreseeable future. It never crossed my mind it would merely be a stepping stone to the next destination, a mile marker on the highway of my life. Brussels felt like home. I had a place in this world, and I didn't see a reason to seek another, not at least until I met my husband.

From our very first date we shared a hunger. We desired a life out on the edge, a global experience that would take us near and far. When we sat in that little Greek café on that rainy Sunday afternoon in Brussels, we painted a road map of places we not only wanted to visit but possible places we would have interest in living. When the opportunity presented itself that we could look at the map and relocate, I didn't know what to think. My future plans had only taken into account Belgium. After leaving Phoenix, I really didn't reconfigure my three, five and/or ten-year goals like I had done in the past. For the most part, I was living day by day, organically discovering new opportunities and embracing the twists and turns along the way. I had no particular destination in mind, and my goals were obtainable within the parameters of a year or two.

I had really only just got my bearings when I met Bartosz. Life had finally started to get easier abroad. I was now used to my adopted country, its quirky rules, and its way of life. From filing insurance claims by directly mailing or dropping off the doctor's bill to the office to registering at the Town Hall and having the police come to my residence to confirm my address when I moved. I wasn't quite sure if I wanted to roll the dice again and start all over from scratch. My papers were in order, and I could work for myself as an independent. Change, as exciting as it is and was at the time, is also consuming. I am always the first one to advocate for change, knowing full well the extent of what I am getting into. It takes energy, hard work and perseverance. A major life change is not a decision you take lightly without weighing the pros and cons, and the options. I had taken the leap of faith on my own, and I wasn't quite sure how we would transition together as a couple. Would it be easier or more difficult being two and not just one? There was no doubt in my mind it would be far from easy. Change ultimately leads to uncertainty and, as a newlywed couple, we would embark on an adventure that could test our marriage and our future together.

As the big moving day approached, we decluttered our fifth-floor walkup in downtown Brussels. When we first met, nine months earlier, Bartosz was in the process of moving. He went from a 100-meter square apartment in the more dominantly Flemish-speaking municipality of Brussels Woluwe. He had a Polish friend who had bought the downtown apartment and remodeled it before taking a post in Warsaw. It sat idle until Bartosz decided to downsize knowing it would only be temporary. He had already made up his mind that his time in Brussels was drawing near to an end, and in making this decision, he did not want to maintain a strict contract with Belgian landlords who preferred having 3-year lease agreements.

We would be leaving the tiny cobblestone streets and amazing views of the historic Grand Place for the more organized and cleaner, more modern city of Barcelona. We arranged the must-haves and tossed the rubbish. It was unbelievable the things I had accumulated in the short period of time I had lived in Belgium. I had moved from my tiny 35-meter, one bedroom flat into the attic of an old townhouse where Bartosz lived. I had rid myself once of furnishings, clothes, excess clutter, only to regain a multitude of things I just didn't need anymore. It is no joke when they say there is an "art" of living with less and appreciating it.

After 25 trips up and down the stairs, my body was exhausted. Muscles I never knew I had were screaming with agony. We loaded the moving van, the two of us, in five hours and set off as the sun was beginning to set below the horizon. I said goodbye to a place that will always hold a fond place in my heart. With a long thirteen-hour drive ahead of us, we set off into the night. Heading south, we were about to start again.

Autumn in Barcelona is rainy, a bit brisk and a little solemn. Although it is a city inundated by hordes of tourists, it becomes quieter as the summer fades and the cooler temperatures set in.

We started on the task I was all too familiar with by now. Shopping for furniture and fixtures that would create a welcoming, comfortable space for both of us to reside. It was no longer his and hers, but ours and our various styles had to collide under one roof. We had left all of our major furniture back in the flat in Brussels, and it allowed us to start with an undefined space ready for design. You may be wondering then what we had actually packed in the moving van if the furniture stayed behind? It's quite funny because I kept pointing out the fact since European apartments typically lack closets we needed a lot of storage, which meant armoires, ornate boxes, shelves, anything that could tidy the mess. We are both avid adventure sport enthusiasts and, with that passion, comes equipment and apparel. Snowboards, boots, bindings, kite equipment, it all had to find a place, tucked away from the everyday eye.

In a long list of things to do from establishing utilities to getting Spanish phones numbers, we managed to arrange furniture and have it delivered. All before the second week passed, we were up and operational, no longer living out of suitcases and cardboard boxes. We could start focusing on the other more important details such as the paperwork. The dreaded process never ceases to amaze me, every country a little different, but no less frustrating and time-consuming. The process is like a shadow that is never lost but lingers behind every corner and turn you take.

I left a few details out here. How on earth would I go through the whole employment procurement process again? That was essentially what I would have had to do in order to stay in Spain and essentially the EU. Since I was moving, I had to forfeit my permits in Belgium and start over. How could I do that to myself? I had just got the golden ticket in Brussels, and I returned it to start with a blank slate.

Well, things had changed in fact. You heard me say husband, yes? We were married in October, and by November we had moved. My Polish prince charming and I got married, and not for immigration purposes but for that heart-throbbing, can't live without him kind of love. I would never had made that big of a life decision to merely make moving more manageable. What it ultimately came down to was that we were in love. Our hopes and ambitions fell in line with one another, and we could see a future together. It never happened like that before with anyone else.

When I closed my eyes, I could see our lives, five, ten years down the road, and it was remarkable. We would continue to grow together, and our relationship would flourish having children and creating a family. We would be grandma and grandpa relaxing on a porch swing in heaven knows what country telling exaggerated stories to our grandchildren. Maybe I am getting ahead of myself here, but what was the purpose of waiting? Marriage would always be a gamble, there's no predetermined equation that can define a perfect marriage and if it will end up working out. Coming from a family that was wrecked by divorce I never thought I would believe in the coming together of two souls forever and forever, death do us part, but I was willing to seek it out, and take a chance on love. Why not give our fairytale romance a shot?

It didn't really matter whether we had been together for eight months or ten years when he got down on one knee on a rooftop terrace overlooking a skyline of city lights. We were in Barcelona for my birthday back in August visiting some friends and staying in their penthouse apartment.

On my 29th birthday we hopped into our rented SUV and headed to the designer outlet shops at La Roca Village to find a special cocktail dress for the evening's festivities before making our way north to Girona. Stopping over in this medieval city for lunch, we sat down to a late afternoon selection of delightful tapas paired with local wine before strolling the grounds of the Benedictine monastery of Sant Pere de Galligants. Making our way along its wall-top promenade, we relished in the magnificent view of Sant Feliu church, Girona's first cathedral dating back to the 10th century. From the old city center, we made a coastal drive along the Mediterranean stopping in Lloret de Mar where we found a quaint little seaside bungalow offering coffee before returning just before nightfall to the city.

Reservations had been made over a month in advance for Ferran and Albert Adria's Tickets located in Barcelona's old theatre district. I was told to freshen up before dinner and to meet Bartosz on the terrace for a glass of cava, Spanish sparkling wine, my favorite of all bubbly! I gently pulled on my emerald green dress with brushed silver metal beading and slipped my feet into black leather stilettos I had packed for the occasion.

Bartosz was waiting with two crystal flutes. Handing me the glasses, he asked me to turn and face the city. Wondering what he was doing behind my back, I heard him say he would be back in a minute. I had an inkling that I knew what he was up to, but he came back with a metal knife in his hand, not quite what I was expecting. He was struggling to pop the cork from the bottle.

Fumbling with the metal wire buried into the cork that wrapped around the glass neck, he finally released the cork into the air. I am sure that was nerve-wracking knowing now what was yet to come. It's not every day you ask your sweetheart for their hand in marriage. I could be naïve and say I had no idea, yes, the whole trouble cracking the bottle open wasn't part of the plan, but it added suspense. Coming to my side, he poured the two glasses and set the bottle on the ground next to the railing. He turned me to face the city and asked me to close my eyes. Seconds passed, and he wrapped his arms around me and turned me back to face him with a diamond ring held in his hand. Nervously he asked the question, "Will you marry me?" And without hesitation, from our very first date, it was always going to be "yes."

My family may have thought we were crazy, but I think they were getting used to my nonconventional antics by now. At least we didn't elope in Vegas and keep it a secret. We returned to the United States in October just as the trees were changing color alight in auburn-reds and chestnut hues. My dress was made of shimmering gold sequence melting into the autumnal milieu, standing next to my handsome husband dressed in a sleek navy blue suit as we walked to the county courthouse late in the afternoon. We did not don the traditional attire, because it was meant to be an informal affair. My father and brother, dressed in their Sunday best, served as witnesses. We would delay the formal religious ceremony and reception until June back in Bartosz's hometown Gdansk.

After signing our marriage license, we held a very small, yet charming gathering with my family. What meant the most was that my grandmother from my mother's side, whom I worked with in the roadside diner over a decade ago, was present. She too, among so many, had battled cancer and overcame it, only to be re-diagnosed a year later. She was putting up a great fight, but I knew she would not be able to make the trek to Poland in her condition to see her oldest granddaughter all in white.

The whole trip had been organized last minute. We bought tickets the night before we flew out of Amsterdam Schiphol into Cedar Rapids, Iowa. With little in the way of proper planning, it all fell into place. Even the owner and chef of the bistro, a family friend, went ahead without our asking and made two one-tier wedding cakes with an array of small fresh wildflowers of vibrant violet, canary yellow and magenta delicately arranged around the edge of the ivory buttercream frosting. Lemon cake with black currant puree and vanilla with a soft Bavarian cream, the whole evening was magical. With both our families' blessings, we were embarking on this amazing journey.

We opted for a neutral space that was neither his land nor my land. We compromised, and we agreed we would start our life as newlyweds in Spain. We knew there would be hurdles and that life would be full of unexpected surprises, but at least we were in it together.

Being married to a citizen of the European Union, I would have to say made the whole immigration process look like child's play considering the ringer I had been through in Belgium. Maybe I was just an old veteran at it by now, but I beg to differ. I was so used to having multiple copies, translations and apostilles that I prepared for more than I needed. We went into the Office for Foreigners after my husband registered in Spain. With a red folder in hand filled with licenses, identification numbers and certificates, we were ready. Everything that I had submitted before, a background check, copies of diplomas, transcripts and birth records. The woman that took our number was surprised by our organization. We were accompanied by a Polish friend who was married to a Catalan and operated a Polish/Spanish Info Point. He offered his services to help assist us if our meager level of Spanish was lacking.

The whole meeting took less than ten minutes. She flipped through our documents, taking the ones she needed and filled out a receipt. The folder would be submitted to the Director of the Office of Foreigners who would take a decision. We would be contacted within thirty days if our application had been approved or rejected.

Simple. The whole process of hurry up and wait wasn't new.

We passed the time. A few friends originally from Argentina and the Netherlands had been living in Barcelona for a few years and were knowledgeable about the hip and trendy places only the locals go to. This insider scoop made it easier to get to know the city, tapping into their experiences and taking advice where it was needed.

I confess that it was much more difficult to make new friends being a couple than on my own. Being single had its advantages just as much as being in a relationship, but I did find I didn't expand my network as quickly in Barcelona as I had in Brussels. Maybe it was the language and the concentration of expats. Barcelona was not Brussels, and it wasn't trying to be.

A country hit far worse by the economic crisis, Spaniards were more conservative. Business was much slower, and the spirit of entrepreneurship was there but it didn't have the same high energy thrust to be something great like it is in Brussels or in the United States for that matter. It was just different.

I didn't have a job like I had landed in Brussels, which made my circle of contacts much smaller. We were very outgoing, but we had been out in the expat scene for some time, and nothing really changed. It was the same old set of questions and monotonous responses that sounded like a pre-recorded voiceover. Parties where you felt like you were in a meat market being prodded did not appeal to us.

It wasn't until we started to really get involved in language courses, training at the gym and going to yoga classes that we started to break away from the very introverted life we were shaping for ourselves.

I'm not quite sure how we fell into a rut, secluding ourselves from the outside world (I wouldn't go so far to say we were extrovert, but something in between. Ambivert is what they call it). When we wanted to be social, we were, and when we wanted a quiet night home, we were just as happy. Whereas before we were beginning to look like hermits, we dug our way out of our shells.

Life was different. Eating a late lunch, having a siesta in the middle of the afternoon and going for dinner at ten o'clock at night was a change. I once heard someone say, "The day starts in Spain when it ends in Germany." When citizens from Northern European countries are packing it in and snuggling into their beds at night, Barcelona residents are heading out to restaurants, bars and cafes to wine and dine. There is a specific energy about the city and its people that other cities can aspire to.

We were learning the rules of the land and trying to abide. We had to create some adaptations to fit our schedules and created a hybrid which seemed to work. We found a welcomed balance that neither one of us had experienced in our constantly on-the-go, busy lives we had lived before. It took longer than I anticipated, but slowly Barcelona started to feel like home and Brussels would eventually turn into a lingering memory, a benchmark identifying where I had been and where I was going.

My friends' presence in Barcelona was a capstone. Their visit from the United States allowed me to once and for all close the door on my past and leave it there. In one of our conversations Lana told me Joshua and his fiancé split up. Not that I relished in this news, I don't wish heartache on anyone, but a little piece of me felt like karma had its place and that was enough. Phoenix, Brussels, and now Barcelona, I was gaining wisdom, and my brain was swimming in an ocean of new knowledge that I wanted to share. I guess having some downtime had its perks. I could now unearth my new life's discoveries to find purpose in a city that was now my own.

WISDOM | TRANSITIONS

Life was a flurry of change, and in the midst of the storm, the only thing that could keep me grounded and sane was to live in the moment.

We have all heard the popular saying *when one door closes, another one opens*. In life, we may have all experienced this in some way or another. The quiet lull into we which we transition to between ideas, projects and goals can make life seem empty. After accomplishing one milestone, you may want to move immediately onto the next. However, when your next step is unclear, you may feel frustrated, disconnected or fall into a mild depression. You may even identify your lack of forward momentum as falling behind.

Anxiety mounting, I've been there many times.

To ease these troubling thoughts, try to look at it from a different angle. If your intention is personal growth, you will continue to grow as an individual, whether you are working toward a specific objective or not. Spending time engrossed by the ebb and flow of life can be a liberating experience that gives you the time you need to think about what you have recently undergone and contemplate what direction to take next.

The mindful transitional pause can take many forms depending upon the situation. For some, it can be a period of reflection on the past and how it has unfolded. For others, it can be a period of adjustment, where new values are shaped and integrated into daily life. Don't stress. Just because you are not running full force to the finish line doesn't mean you should presume that you have lost your stride. The period between here and there can become a wonderful time of contentment that readies you for the next chapter that will soon be unveiled.

Whatever is on the next page, it requires you to be bigger and better than you were before. It requires a transformation within us that sometimes we do not even acknowledge is taking place.

CHAPTER 16

DEFINITIONS

"Accept no one's definition of your life; define yourself."
-Harvey Fierstein

As a couple, we were in a peculiar position, we didn't really have jobs or any form of employment. I wanted to be my own boss, and my husband was taking some much-deserved time off to rest and redirect his energy splitting his time between Spain and Poland, brainstorming ideas of what he wanted to do next as far as his career was concerned. It would seem like we had it all. Well not exactly, what we had was an opportunity, a chance to combine our talents and ambitions in a way that would set the tone for our future together. But for all intents and purposes, we were between here and there. One project had finished, and the next was yet to begin; we had left great careers and were now, what was it, that dreaded word, yes… unemployed.

"Unemployed," what an ugly word!

Imagine you answered a complete stranger or a friend of a friend, 'I am unemployed.' What tone would you set for the conversation? Would the other person have pity, or look down on you as a nobody? In the United States, we Americans tend to be obsessed with titles and the dividends associated to them. We wager part of a person's worth by what they do from nine to five and how much they earn. Whether it is right or wrong, we judge one another in that fashion.

As time went by, my husband and I started to look at our lives differently. If this moment in time was such a blessing, why were we tearing ourselves down? I call it a blessing because yes, we were unemployed, but there was no immediate rush to accept a new position or tackle a new undertaking if it wasn't well-grounded and researched properly. We had time and yes, more importantly, enough money to support ourselves in the interim. Bartosz left a well-paid position working for the European political institutions, and I still had my savings to fall back on. There was no better time to rewrite our course than the present.

The first thing on our to-do list was to make a much-needed change in our elevator pitch. We were the authors of our own novel, and we could write whatever version of the truth we wanted to tell. Our story was ours to compose, and we could disclose what facts that were pertinent. We didn't change the truth, but we adapted our story to be more forward-moving focusing on the positive rather than the negatives in our situation. Yes, we were unemployed, but what many would consider a set-back afforded us time to study, to read, to travel, to meet new people, and to experience Spanish culture. Changing our verbatim gave us a whole new perspective and started to create a more affirmative image that not only attracted new friendships but made us more confident going through the transitional period.

We had been living in Barcelona for three or four months when I received an email from a gentleman in San Francisco, California. Taking a leisure trip, he was flying into Barcelona for the weekend before he launched his new company. Dan had found my contact information as a yoga instructor on the web and decided to shoot me an email about a week before he was scheduled to arrive to see if I could offer any advice on studios or particular classes he could participate in.

Getting back in touch with Dan, I invited him, and he accepted to join a Sunday morning class I offered that had started to become somewhat of a ritual for the small community of students I had established. We would spend an hour on the mat and go out for brunch at any one of our many favorite local eateries that dotted the city. It was a fun, energetic way to start the day and allow students to build relationships with one another.

Running back from the bakery, I had a fresh loaf of bread and a gym bag in my hand when I met Dan. It had been a busy Sunday morning running around, and I hardly made a good first impression. He was punctual, I was not. The first to arrive, this extra time gave us an opportunity to chat about his yoga experience and what brought him to Barcelona. Right from the start, there was a deep connection and a sense of empathy with Dan that I had only ever found with students that I had been teaching for several months. Within a few minutes, I had a good grasp of Dan's current situation. He had told me about his life back in San Francisco and a period of change he was transitioning through.

His professional story was not so different from mine, even though we worked in vastly different industries. Exchanging our notes, I learned he had been working for an IT company and had quit six months earlier. He was unemployed by conventional standards, and he had a non-compete clause in his contract that prohibited him joining a similar company or to participate in like activities as performed in his previous job. The clause also meant that his clients were off-limits for a predetermined amount of time as well.

Tough would only begin to scratch the surface of the trials he went through after making the decision to leave his job. He didn't have a glossy preconceived image that leaving his job would be easy, but he was taken aback by the things that he was never prepared to confront. Come to find out what troubled him wasn't what I had expected at all.

Dan had just started dating a new man, and he was going through all the motions, falling in love, the infatuation, the newness found in every moment together. It wasn't the relationship that was concerning. They would go to house parties together, and he would introduce himself as recently unemployed. It took his boyfriend pulling him aside to tell him that he was making a poor first impression. "But why?" A bit puzzled at first, he thought, "unemployed" that was it. That word was what made people cringe and feel uneasy around him. A word with such power and stigma that it has the ability to make the person in question feel less worthy, or not good enough, not smart enough. Of course, the easy way out would be to say that, "Hey, I am just taking a sabbatical," but that wasn't the truth. Dan wasn't being paid to take this time off. Yes, he may have decided to leave the company he had worked for, but the non-compete clause was limiting him as to what he could do in the meantime. There was good reason for his boyfriend's concern.

Yes, Dan wasn't employed, but it was by his own choice. He consciously left his position and was taking this period to start his own business. Rather than expending his time and energy in a company where he didn't feel he was making a difference, he wanted to make a change going out on his own. The momentary delay that the non-compete clause provided was an adequate time frame to lay the groundwork for his new endeavor without formally launching the company to the public and being in violation of his old contract. He would abide by the constraints of his former employer, but that was not to say he was sitting idle counting down the days, twiddling his fingers until he could go back to work. He was busy and more energetic than ever working on his own ambitions finding the balance between working in an office environment and out on one's own, either in coffee shops or in his home which was very different. He needed more structure, so he learned how to provide that for himself using various tools such as finding a co-working space, setting hours in which he would work from home and those he could run errands or do laundry. Becoming an entrepreneur presents its own set of challenges from social interactions to working without distraction.

I could empathize with Dan on many levels. When I left the spa as a yoga instructor, I was also hindered to continue my professional activity for a term of eighteen months. Outrageous right!? Dan was given six months as an IT manager, and I, a mere yoga instructor, had to wait a year and a half before pursuing my career again. Well, not to get too into the details, I wasn't going to accept this extreme of a sentence and had a lawyer get involved to check the validity of the contract. After close review and analyzing Belgian employment regulations, the non-compete clause in my contract was actually deemed void, but it didn't mean I couldn't relate to the position Dan was in.

Time was on his side, but it was what he did with this time that served to define him. Once his boyfriend pointed the issue out to Dan, he started to look deeper into how he expressed himself to others. He understood it was all within the mind. He had control over what he said and how he felt about the situation, the transition he was going through. He started to identify with the tasks he was tackling building his new business, and before he realized it, the time passed, and he found himself in Barcelona days before he would launch his company.

It was so enlightening to be able to empathize with another American on this issue, how we define ourselves. Looking at other people's lives, you never understand the issues they are working through. We imagine everyone has it all figured out, but that's never the case. It was refreshing to know someone else was going through a similar dilemma. I guarantee there are many more of us out there.

Words are just that, words. They serve to define us, yes, but we can select the ones we use to create the picture of ourselves we present to others. In the few minutes leading up to the other students joining us for yoga, I learned so much about Dan and myself. It wasn't until Dan's boyfriend pulled him aside did he come to realize that he was presenting an unfair image of himself to others. For so long, he had got used to telling people what he did for a living as a means to depict the type of person he was. But Dan was so much more than a title. He had recently started his yoga practice. He was an avid traveler and loved the San Francisco food scene. There were so many other interests and hobbies that he could use to express himself, not to mention his exciting new business endeavor!

It isn't until we share what we are going through with others do we come to realize we are not so dissimilar or alone in our pursuits. What a happy coincidence, a moment of serendipity having met Dan. From San Francisco to Barcelona, he was put into my life to teach me a lesson I had only begun to comprehend on my own. My husband and I faced our own variation of a similar transition having left our lives and the old definitions of who we were back in Brussels. In this new home we were creating, we had the extraordinary opportunity to select the words, interests and projects we would undertake that would create a better image, a more well-rounded picture, of the individuals we were to become.

WISDOM 1 WHAT'S IN A LABEL?

How do you define yourself? By your title, profession, role in the family, or is it something bigger? Take a stark look at yourself and move past the references that only seem to scratch the surface. You are so much more than what meets the eye.

As humans, we have the tendency to name and categorize people, places and things. Every creature on earth carries or has carried some label, such as young, old, musician, painter, animal advocate, parent, child or liberal, that either they, themselves or others used to define them. While labels establish useful first impressions, they can also act as a tall barrier between the world and ourselves. Expectations stem from labels. When individuals begin to define others in terms of their profession, looks, wealth or political background, it becomes tougher to accept them unconditionally. This is two-fold. When we assign ourselves a label, we limit ourselves and our potential by effectively pigeonholing our identities. The task then lies in finding a balance between that which serves to define us and our nature to grow and evolve with time.

Learning first who we are as children, our identities are forged by society, which labels us so-and-so's children, a boy or a girl, a nerd or a jock, or an introvert or an extrovert. This is innate, considering that characterizing others upon first meeting is an automatic process as we saw in this chapter. It is when we regard these initial impressions as unchangeable that we deny the fact that we are all blessed with roles that can change from day to day or exist simultaneously. It is possible to be a parent, an author, a swimmer and an entrepreneur all at once. If you were to choose a single role, such as being an accountant, it would limit the paths you could take. But if you define yourself by saying you are a creative person, you have many more avenues to explore to channel that creativity.

We are so much more than what we do or what we have done in the past. Everyone on this earth is capable of taking on a new identity or letting go of an old one. It is your choice. You may choose to be "a strong-mannered executive" in one period of your life and "a nurturing parent" in another. Yet you remain wholly you.

Labels have the potential to be a good stepping off point, but they do not replace our understanding of who we really are. If everyone was encouraged to look beyond labels, open-mindedness and tolerance would be the inevitable outcome. Wouldn't that be nice?

Think about it, honestly and openly, who are you?

CHAPTER 17

DREAMING WITH EYES WIDE OPEN

"Every great dream begins with a dreamer. Always remember, you have it within you the strength, the patience, and the passion to reach for the stars..."
–Harriet Tubman

Polish was the main language of communication. Listening intently wasn't a problem, I had done this for a while now, trying to decipher and quickly pick out the words I knew that would give some clue as to what the conversation was about. It was all about context I realized. If I could relate to the story being told, it was much easier to be involved or at least stay somewhat engaged in the conversation without blanking out and staring off into space.

I had been studying Polish for over six months, but my comprehension had not yet risen above a three-year-old child's capacity. It was both a frustrating and rewarding process. Of course I wanted to communicate, but learning a language plain and simply takes time and practice. Getting the hang of it, my vocabulary was expanding, but forming complete sentences was trying. I didn't have the pesky inhibitions I had had once before having tried learning French or German for that matter. I wanted to learn this language, and that made all the difference.

Confidently, I gave it my best shot, knowing full well I would butcher what it was I was trying to say, but it didn't matter. I felt comfortable. No one mocked or ridiculed me if my pronunciation wasn't quite right. Once I even said, "Maybe I could borrow the pretty man," confusing everyone in the room, when what I was trying to ask was, "May I borrow your white scarf?" What came out was similar in sound but far from the same meaning, causing a roar of congenial laughter.

The company that I kept, family and friends, cheered me on, hoping I would succeed, and someday, a day a very long way away, I would become fluent in Polish. That day wasn't today, but oh how my new family I married into wished it were. They couldn't wait to know more about me, to ask me questions and learn about my past. I too had questions that would be left unanswered until another day.

Every time we got together with Bartosz's family, we were able to learn a little more about one another. They were that type of people, engaging, friendly and inquisitive. From the very first moment I met his mother, I felt a welcomed place in her heart. It had been an incessantly cold night in early spring. Bartosz and I had only been dating a few months. Flying into Warsaw late one evening, Bartosz picked me up in his car he had driven up from Lublin in the south of Poland. He was taking a long weekend away from the political campaign he was working on. We made the nearly four-hour drive north to Gdansk racing along the back-country roads through tiny villages until we saw the lights of the old shipyards in the distance, a very distinctive feature of the seaside city along the Baltic. When he could see the glow from the distance, he knew he was home. Having been to Poland before, as I mentioned, much of what I saw was familiar, but this visit would be different, even more exciting. I was meeting the parents.

When we pulled into the drive parking just outside the iron fence that surrounded the property, we saw the light turn on above the door to the downstairs guest apartment. It was a little past midnight, and they were still awake, expecting our arrival. Before we had time to ring the doorbell, his mother came running out into the near-freezing cold in her nightgown and slippers. Turning the keys and opening the gate, she swept right past her son to give me a warm embrace. Without words, I could feel her gentle kindness, that sort of motherly love that I had been long out of touch with.

I still have that same feeling every time we visit his family. They all have this same effect, every member, aunt, uncle, sister, even his niece Nadia has this way of making me feel welcome in a land that is not my own. They make you feel like one of them, never an outsider, never a foe. Maybe it is bred in their culture? I have heard it said, but there is something special to be admired about Polish hospitality; it is truly one of a kind. From having a feast prepared on the table to share with their guests or having a pair of slippers to offer when you enter their home, there is no lack of goodwill and kindness. My mother-in-law once even gave me the furry slippers she was wearing because she thought I was cold. Any differences that could separate are washed away, and you are made to feel a part of the bigger whole.

Months had passed since our first meeting. It wasn't quite yet Christmas, but the joy of the season was ever-present. Bartosz had business to attend, and I was content on spending quality time with his family. It was the eve of Saint Nicholas, December 6th, when we all gathered around the dinner table. The extended family, the aunts and the uncles, even Bartosz's godparents made it for the occasion. We had raced off to get married in the United States, a quick, unceremonious affair months earlier and I was the new addition, the new Mrs. in the house, and it was about time to make the formal introductions.

The evening in my eyes could not have been more enchanting. The snow falling outside, frost glistening on the window panes, the smell of smoked meats and freshly baked bread danced through the air. His mother had hung a beautiful garland from one of the wood beams above the table decorated with handmade white lace doilies and silver ornaments. A fresh cut evergreen stood as a focal point in the center of the room between the dining table and the sitting area with the luminous glow of soft white lights. I hadn't had a Christmas like this in years! It was like I had stepped back in time before my parents' divorce, a time of yesteryear. Memories of Thanksgivings and Christmas's spent at my grandparents cozied up by the fire. I had this overwhelming sense of nostalgia that gave me butterflies. I felt like a little child with her stool pulled up next to her grandmother, making gingerbread men for Santa, drinking eggnog and looking out at the snow-covered pasture beyond the window sill. Fond memories of a faraway place in an even more remote moment in time.

As the guests arrived, I was taken aback by everyone's enthusiasm to get to know me. The gentlemen of the family kissed my hands, and the ladies pulled me in tight with three kisses to either cheek. I could smell their floral perfume, and it smelled like my own aunts and grandmother had been transported across lands. Bartosz was doing his very best, trying to translate every word from Polish to English and back again. Whew, what a task! It wasn't easy, with a light heart and enthusiasm he wanted his family to know his bride.

That was the beginning of a new chapter. For so long, I was left out on my own, not for want or desire, but because I needed to move through life at my own pace. I needed to learn and discover things about myself and about the world around me before I could get to this place of peace. Family, a word that had little meaning to me after my parents' divorce, was now brought back to life in vivid color. It had value and a warmth that felt reassuring.

That is not to say that I didn't have my own family back in the United States that loved and supported me, they did. My father lived in Iowa, and my mother lived in Phoenix. They never spoke. My relatives crisscrossed the American countryside East to West, North to South. Living in Phoenix, I hardly had the opportunity to return for family reunions and holidays, my job just didn't allow it. I was always that family member who needed to reintroduce myself, not like they forgot about me, but the distance separated us, and we had little knowledge of what each other's daily life was like. The frame of reference we had was that I had my life, and they had theirs.

This does not sadden me. My past is just that, the past. I now can embrace the present without taking for granted what for some may be so commonplace. Having close family and friends by my side before was rare. I had friends, yes and at some point, my ex had played a major part of my life, but I eventually had to face the truth that these individuals I had chosen to surround myself with were not the most understanding, nor did they have the tools to support my outside-the-box thinking. I have had to learn to accept it. I learned that I can and should choose more appropriately those with whom I surround myself. It is not that these people from my past didn't love me or have my best interest at heart, but what may have felt like lack of support may have been their way of trying to protect me. I always wondered what exactly they were protecting me from, myself or my dreams. It was unfortunate that we didn't see the world in the same frame of light.

From Belgium to Spain, and from a handful of other countries on the road map, I now had a wealth of friends and an adoptive family that gave me the support I had been looking for. It was when I stepped out on the world's stage, out on the edge in the face of fear that I felt safer and more assured than I had ever felt before when I lived inside my comfort zone.

Setting a date, we were planning a second wedding celebration, a more formal affair considering the first was a bit sporadic and last minute. We had compromised. The first wedding had no flowers or violins ushering us down the aisle, just two witnesses and a civil servant finalizing our marital agreement. The second wedding would be the type that is written down in fables. A big white Polish wedding may be a little exaggerated, but it wasn't far from the truth. The second wedding was a juncture in the road that would bring my two worlds together on one stage in Gdansk. I was excited. This momentous occasion was not only a celebration of our love, of course, that was of utmost importance, but for me, it was even more than that. It meant that I would have the opportunity to show my family, those that could make the long flight, that my gamble wasn't so outlandish in respect to their initial thoughts when I sold off my life's belongings on a chance, on a wishful dream to create the life I had envisioned for myself. I could ease their minds of stress and worry, reassuring them that even though I now lived thousands of miles away, I was in good hands. I was no longer wandering lost in the night. I had found my place in the light safe and sound.

It was a fusion of culture and tradition, between the United States and Poland. We worked long and hard on finding common ground, emails back and forth to vendors, cake tastings and dress fittings, all in a language I could hardly speak. No one ever tells you how stressful weddings can become, not to mention on the international stage where both parties have different expectations and communication is limited. I cannot nor do I want to relive the many heated arguments and frustrated conversations Bartosz and I had trying to find a mutual consensus.

On our way to pick up my wedding dress in Gdynia, one of the cities that comprised the Tricity area along the Baltic, we got into it, saying things we didn't mean that resulted in tears falling down my cheeks and Bartosz saying it was over. It was over, we both were in shock. Was it for real, is that what we wanted? Bartosz kept driving. The car was silent. We got to Gdynia, and I was dropped off in front of the dress shop. I walked in with puffy eyes, unable to hide the hurt.

Bartosz returned after parking and still not a word was said. It wasn't until we were on our way back that we called a truce and decided with the wedding dress hanging in the back seat that we both overreacted.

There are a few testaments I arrived at from this experience. One, men do not take wedding planning nearly as seriously as women do. It was not my fault, but my inability to speak the language put an unanticipated strain on our relationship up until the final days. Very close to calling things off we had to have space, emotions raged from a place of frustration and lack of understanding.

It was by the gracious kindness of Bartosz's mother and his sister that everything fell into its rightful place but not before we had created a few more memories.

When it came to sending out invitations, I would say I had high hopes at first that I would have a large audience to witness the exchange of our vows, but I quickly started to get real with the truth that I was asking a lot from my friends and family from the States. I was asking them to take time out of their lives, their jobs, and we all know Americans cannot get that much time off work to go gallivanting around. Not to mention the expense of traveling thousands of miles would take its toll on the pocketbook.

Okay, I got it. I wasn't terribly happy, but then again on the bright side, I had a wonderful array of friends not but a few short flights away living in Europe that could make the trek.

After the flights for my father, grandmother and brother had been booked, I felt that that was enough. I even invited my mother, not knowing what her response would be. I wasn't surprised frankly even though I was persistent in asking. I insisted she would live to regret not coming to her only daughter's wedding, but everyone has their own decisions to make. The excuse rested on cost, it was too much to spend. Too much to spend on what would be a single moment in time you would never get a repeat performance of?! Well, I leave it there.

I couldn't expect so much from others, but it meant the world to me to have these three individuals at my side. They represented where I came from. They had played such a quintessential role in my past that it was important to me that they also be present at this new beginning.

We were late getting to the airport. My father and grandmother had arrived two hours before our train would even enter the city of Warsaw. We had to rearrange our train tickets when we received a message from my brother that my grandmother and father were held up in Toronto. Before my father departed Canada the following day we spoke, and I had given him strict instructions where we should meet. I had specifically told him to sit and have lunch at the hotel that was adjacent to the airport. It would be hard to miss, not but a five-minute walk from the arrivals gate. They would have time to relax after their nine-hour flight, and we would arrive shortly thereafter to take them to the hotel we had booked in the city. A simple instruction, at least that was what I had thought. Yet when we arrived, they were nowhere to be found! We searched high and low, from the arrivals gate to check-in, departures, looking at every lounge area, café and coffee shop, talking with airport security and immigration control, and no one had seen them. I couldn't even get confirmation from the airline they were flying with that they had even arrived in Warsaw, this being their final destination. Talking to the airline service agents, there was no way to retrieve my own family's information from their records. I was at a loss of what to do. For hours, we walked the airport scavenging high and low looking for clues as to where they could be. I have to confess I don't lose my composure very often, but standing at the airline information counter, I was having a heated argument with the agent that stood across from me. I, myself, had purchased these airline tickets for my family, and I was still denied pertinent information that could help in our search!

The past few days had been a little unnerving. My father and grandmother were supposed to arrive 24 hours earlier, but they were held up in Toronto unable to catch their flight because of a delay out of Chicago O'Hare. Go figure, I always have trouble there. They had been traveling for two days straight, and we lost them. This was hardly the warm welcome to Poland I had anticipated.

Not knowing what further action to take, whether to file a missing person report or not, we resolved to go to our hotel and wait for some shred of hope. Maybe they would try to contact us.

The past week had seemed like a never-ending struggle, one thing after another fell out of place, from changing florists to the management of the tables at the reception. What I had thought to have already been arranged and confirmed was readdressed and changed again, making our lives stressful and our fuses short. I was trying not to lose it and break out in tears again. I just kept telling myself it would be okay.

Late in the evening, the taxi pulled up to the curb near the last door leading into the airport. The arrivals gate looked deserted. There was hardly any movement. Planes had long ago dispelled their passengers for the day, and only the janitors inhabited the arrivals hall cleaning the floors of debris. Just before we were about to enter, we spotted two familiar figures sitting in the waiting area on the other side of the glass. My father looked up with tired eyes and despair. I stopped. We had built up so much emotion, frustration, fear and even anger throughout the day that I needed to take a breath. I was trembling. Was it anger or a release of all the built-up emotion? I needed a moment to just be still. Hugging Bartosz, I needed to find my grounding before confronting them.

We entered the hall, not knowing what to expect. Our embraces were not heartwarming but that of strangers, cold and distant. Disheartened and exhausted, you could nearly cut the tension with a blade. Over the two-days of travel, they were in the same clothes as they had been when they boarded their first flight from Cedar Rapids.

Where had they been this entire time? They had arrived over twelve hours before this. On top of an excruciating journey, this had to happen. Setting that aside, we all were a bit testy. Our emotions had run wild. We tried to replay how this mix up could have happened. There was no use in rehashing the days' events, picking at an already salted wound. We had all been upset, and it was time to move on.

It was two days before our big white wedding would commence and we set all of our to-do lists and last-minute preparations aside for a family dinner. The long-awaited moment where my family would finally meet his. I was looking forward to this occasion even more so than the wedding itself in some regard. Not that the white dress didn't factor in there somewhere, but it truly came down to the people involved that were to make this occasion remarkable.

My dad, brother and grandma were all very reserved. They had some travel experience, but being in an international environment socially was not something they had become accustomed to. Not knowing what to expect, they anticipated someone would take the lead. Without hesitation, my mother-in-law swooped in to give my grandmother the most genuine squeeze, she was enamored that someone of my grandmother's age would make such a voyage to be witness to her granddaughter's wedding. I, of course, tried to explain to everyone that my relationship with my grandmother was unlike any other. She was my best friend and confidant. She had played a pinnacle role in my upbringing and would let nothing stand in her way from seeing her oldest granddaughter walk down the aisle. She would have swum through shark-infested waters before raising the white flag. She was a tough woman, and no matter the lengths she would have to travel, she would stand at my side.

The rest of the family joined in and followed suit shaking hands, kissing cheeks, sharing hugs, a mix of Polish and English words were exchanged greeting one another. Before I knew it, my worlds had collided and more so united. What a sensation sitting across from my brother at the dinner table, thinking back to his words coaxing me to follow my dreams, to dispel all reason and go with my instinct. My brother, without fully knowing it, was the root to my happiness. He gave me the courage when I had none. I knew I would find myself out there somewhere and I did, and now my family was there with me, living in my dream.

WISDOM 1 WHEN WORLDS COLLIDE

I have never felt fully American or entirely European. I have felt like this odd commodity sitting on a fence between the lines drawn in the sand. I am proud of my heritage, yet I desire to live life outside the borders of my motherland. Because of this, I find it easier to fit into expat circles where individuals not so dissimilar to me dwell.

I have become accustomed to playing different roles in a variety of companies. I guess it is like being a parent, wife, daughter and professional. We all wear different hats to suit a variety of occasions. When I am in the United States, I try to be that hometown girl next door. I can turn it off and turn it on like a machine. Yet, I feel more comfortable abroad. I am in my element, allowed to live more authentically, eclectically and spontaneously.

When my worlds collided, I felt a new understanding being hatched. Those from the United States got to see the unhindered version of me: a place of being that comes from acceptance. They saw the real me, unadulterated. I wasn't wearing any hat but my own.

For so long, I was searching for my individual identity. After Joshua, I needed to reestablish my unique persona and find a community that would accept me for who I was and not one of the parts I had once played in the past. I found those people in Belgium and throughout my travels abroad. Among them, I felt I was free to be imperfect, to engage unabashedly in communal activities, and to express my vulnerabilities.

The individuals who eventually became my friends are my tribe and out there somewhere in the world your tribe is waiting for you. You are destined to find them, one by one, as you move through life just as I have and continue to do. Sometimes your own efforts will put you in contact with your future tribe members through various projects or events. At other times, circumstances beyond your control will serendipitously spark lifelong connections.

I discovered looking around at the individuals gathered that I was allied with a wonderful and supportive tribe, some old and many new.

However, your life develops after you come together with your tribe, you can be assured that its members will stand at your side. Outwardly your tribe may seem to be nothing more than a loose-knit group of friends and acquaintances to whom you connect with. Yet when you take a closer look, you discover that your tribe gives you roots no matter where in the world you are. They are that foundation that provides you with a sense of community that fulfills many of your basic human needs and supports your ambitions no matter how wild and crazy they may be.

CHAPTER 18

POTENTIAL ABOUNDS

"There are no shortcuts to any place worth going."
-Beverly Sills

Lanterns and topiaries of flowers, soft pink hydrangeas, ivory roses and blush dahlias, flanked the aisle in the church for the performing arts, St. John's, a magnificent vaulted brick cathedral near the Motława River. Dating back to the 1300's it was once a Lutheran Church, and this is my denomination. It was later converted to be a Catholic church, which it remains today, and that is Bartosz's denomination. "How poignant!" Having been burnt and nearly entirely demolished and abandoned after WWII, the Soviets used it as a storehouse for the greater part of the Cold War and Soviet occupation. Since the Solidarity Movement and the fall of communism in Poland, the church has been remarkably restored in part with private funding from those involved in the arts. With its beautiful 12 meter high Renaissance altarpiece and the remains of original tombstones and graves, it stands as one of the great landmarks in Gdansk. It regularly plays host to exhibitions and concerts due to the buildings unique acoustics. With this in mind, our wedding ceremony was scheduled at three in the afternoon to accommodate a later musical performance.

Our guests had arrived by ferry coming across the marina, making a grand entrance into the old city under the arches of the Zuraw, a wooden port crane dating back to 1367. My father, in a charcoal suit, and my brother, in his US Army Dress Blues, squeezed in close making just enough room for the three of us to pass down the aisle as a violinist played Richard Wagner's Bridal Chorus near the altar. Greeted by our priest, he set the tone for the day's celebrations. Speaking in both Polish and English, he fused our two religions throughout the entire ceremony, something we had discussed beforehand making everyone in the audience feel welcome. The musicians, violinist and pianist accompanied by an exquisite female vocalist mesmerized the audience in their rendition of "Ave Maria" in Latin, Oto Baranki Młodi "Here is the young lamb" in Polish and "How Great Thou Art" in English, a more romantic amalgamation of cultures, languages and Christian denominations.

Tradition has it, that at the end of a Polish wedding every guest stands in a line with a bouquet of flowers and gifts for the couple offering kisses to either cheek, wishing their congratulations. Opting to do things our way, we still received our guests but asked them to donate diapers, bottles and formula to a local care center for single mothers and their children. We thought this would be a kind gesture to give back to the community. In addition to this, we were still overwhelmed with flowers and gifts that our best man, my brother and bride's maids accumulated as we embraced our guests.

A remarkably sunny day with temperatures near 90° Fahrenheit, we were incredibly lucky for early June where anything could have been possible. After taking a few last pictures in the church, we jumped into our specially arranged Chevy Cadillac with our photographers and were chauffeured by a porter fit for a role in the Great Gatsby. The city was packed with pedestrians and traffic was jammed. Honking our horn, we had prepared to be stopped by any one of the traditional wedding gates, a group of civilians who make a human barricade restricting the passage of the bride and groom requesting a payment of little airliner vodka bottles. Because of the heat, we did not face such an obstruction, a custom from the Polish countryside.

As our guests returned to the ferry and made their way to the Marina Club Hotel. We arrived at the terrace rooftop greeted by a glass of sparkling wine, bright blue skies, a remarkable view of the Granary Island and old town beyond. Locals and foreigners alike, everyone was impressed by the venue, a brand-new hotel built to overlook the historic city center, taking in the opulent views before we would descend to the Szafarnia 10 Restaurant on the ground floor of the 11-story building. A spacious, modern restaurant with an exposed kitchen and floor to ceiling windows opened to a glass-encased patio and open terrace overlooking the sailboats docked in the marina. Aromas of roasted venison and garlic drifted from the kitchen mingled with the soft perfumes of an array of floral arrangements in antique pink, ivory and lilac nestled next to various vintage glass candle holders and handcrafted menus and place cards. The over six months of planning was executed to perfection. Our cake, a clash of cultures, would not be on display if it were up to the chef, my husband, and his family, but according to my US traditions, the cake is one of the many centerpieces meant to be admired throughout the reception. On this occasion, I was firm in my request and the four-tier masterpiece was set atop a wine barrel. Its base a vanilla cake with bourbon vanilla bean mousse wrapped in ribbons of buttercream frosting which ascended into a chocolate cake with dark chocolate mousse and lemon cake with lemon Bavarian cream and curd, made to look like wood. A two-tone cake with a fresh flower topper and descending flowers and berries that looked like little jewels. I was so happy!

It is hard to imagine looking back that only three years had passed since my relationship with Joshua started to fray, and I was wrecked with grief and hatred at the injustice of it all. I was torn between anger and jealousy. I was jailed by my emotions, and the dark crevices of my mind bubbled and festered like a volcano about to erupt. My friends and loved ones all tried to shower me with kind assurances and uplifting advice, but the darkness within me outcast any light they tried to share. Countless times I was reminded of the old English proverb affirming "time heals all wounds." I would scoff at that in the midst of the pain and agony, but in fact, it was truly all I needed to reconcile my emotions. Time. Finding the strength to travel, to take the time alone on the road in some faraway land was the life-blood I needed to course through my veins.

There was not one definitive moment that I can recall when I finally felt free to live again. It wasn't as though a light switch turned on and all was right in the world, but what had troubled me for so long faded away. I busied myself with things that made me happy. I launched a new career and forced myself to be outgoing and social so much that I had to schedule in "me-time" to just be reflective and mindful of my growth. I was selfish, I won't deny it. I did what I wanted when I wanted with whom I wanted to share my life. I think that was the defining moment when my husband so unexpectedly came into my life. I was in my element. I was attractive and alluring, and

I had this aura about me. Well, maybe it wasn't that blatant, but I had this air of complete confidence that drew him in, like a magnet to metal. I had shifted life into overdrive and went out on my own. I finally started to invest in my own dreams and ambitions. I had let go of the fear of being alone, and I embraced my strength and independence.

I look back, and I see my life as a series of events propelling me forward, each one a building block set atop the last.

Our wedding day was the stepping stone that signified the moment where our lives crossed. I was no longer lost, wandering trying to find my way. I was now an equal part to a greater whole.

That does not go without saying; I would still need to take care of myself to make "us" work moving forward in our life together. I would not find myself down the same pigeon hole again as I had with Joshua giving all of my being to a man without asking for the same in return. I had been there once and speak from experience, it is extremely important to continue to have a voice. Taking care of your own grounding and center of balance will allow you to contribute to the relationship rather than letting the relationship become you.

Reflecting on the past made me become nostalgic. I felt in some regard I had already lived out one full life. If by some freakish accident I would leave this earth tomorrow, I would be satisfied in all I have done. With good fortune, tomorrow will not be my last. I find it hard to imagine I still have my whole life ahead of me and that my journey really has only just begun.

As my family got seated on the train, it started to pull away from the platform. Bartosz and I were left there alone, holding hands looking out into the distance. All the excitement had dissipated, leaving us wondering, what would our next adventure be?

WISDOM I LOVE LIFE HARD

It is so easy to forget the richness in the relationships, experiences, and events that have shaped and define our lives. This may be a result of the unconscious messages we come across daily that cause us to ruminate about what we lack in life or the obstacles we face rather than embrace the abundance we enjoy. As a result, our gratitude and satisfaction in life subsist in constant conflict with our desire for more.

The wealth of gratitude that floods your heart when you come to fully appreciate your abundance may usher in a newfound awareness of the disparity that exists in this world. Be mindful. Taking account of your fortune and how far you have come helps foster a deeper level of appreciation that will allow you to relish and, above all, value your life more fully.

This book has served me to that end. It is a reminder of not only where I have come from but the remarkable journey I have taken to become the woman I am today. I am forever grateful for the ups, downs and turnarounds life has handed me and would not change one page of my story.

NOTE FROM THE AUTHOR

Word-of-mouth is crucial for any author to succeed. If you enjoyed the book, please leave a review online—anywhere you are able. Even if it's just a sentence or two. It would make all the difference and would be very much appreciated.

Thank you!
Emily

ABOUT THE AUTHOR

Emily Szajda, writer, chef, yoga/meditation instructor and sports nutritionist left "Corporate America" for an entrepreneurial life focused on finding work/life balance abroad. She recently returned to the U.S. and lives in Washington DC offering group, corporate and private yoga, meditation and mindfulness trainings in collaboration with recharj® meditation studio and Marino Wellness. Emily provides nutrition counseling to an array of international clients and has appeared on HGTV's House Hunters International and other global media platforms.

IN MEMORIAM

Brent Paliga

Thank you so much for reading one of our
Motivational & Inspirational books.
If you enjoyed our book, please check out our
recommended title for your next great read!

This Side Up by Amy Mangan

A M Y   M A N G A N

This Side Up

The Road to a Renovated Life

A Memoir

"A story of a fighter and fixer. An inspiration to us all."
Carolanne Griffith Roberts, former editor, Southern Living

"This Side Up will leave you feeling relieved, not alone,
hopeful, and grateful for a friend and writer like Amy
Mangan who inspires us to reframe our let downs,
have some laughs, and embrace life with all of its
beautiful unexpected messes." –Stacy Strazis, former
producer The Oprah Winfrey Show and CNN

View other Black Rose Writing titles at
www.blackrosewriting.com/books and use promo
code
PRINT to receive a **20% discount** when purchasing.

CPSIA information can be obtained
at www.ICGtesting.com
Printed in the USA
JSHW010702271219
3202JS00001B/1

9 781684 334117